399073

muAmcC
760009

**IF LUST PLEASE
RETURN TO:**
JAMES VICTORE
36 SOUTH 4TH ST, STUDIO D3
BROOKLYN, NYC 11211 /USA

WITHDRAWN

Pierre Bernard

Mary

R. Venko
.......march2010

D1349720

Fernando Gutiérrez

FANNY LE BRAS

WIL FREEBORN 2009

university for the **creative arts**

Epsom
Ashley Road
Epsom
Surrey
KT18 5BE

Tel: 01372 202461
Fax: 01372 202457
e-mail:libraryepsm@ucreative.ac.uk

LUST

ROCKPORT

741.
6
LUS

© 2011 by Rockport Publishers, Inc.

All rights reserved. No part of this book may be reproduced in any form without written permission of the copyright owners. All images in this book have been reproduced with the knowledge and prior consent of the artists concerned, and no responsibility is accepted by producer, publisher, or printer for any infringement of copyright or otherwise, arising from the contents of this publication. Every effort has been made to ensure that credits accurately comply with information supplied. We apologize for any inaccuracies that may have occurred and will resolve inaccurate or missing information in a subsequent reprinting of the book.

First published in the United States of America by
Rockport Publishers, a member of
Quayside Publishing Group
100 Cummings Center
Suite 406-L
Beverly, Massachusetts 01915-6101
Telephone: (978) 282-9590
Fax: (978) 283-2742
www.rockpub.com

Library of Congress Cataloging-in-Publication Data

Victore, James, 1962-
 Lust : a collaborative art journal from the world's most creative graphic designers / James Victore.
     p. cm.
 Includes bibliographical references and index.
 ISBN-13: 978-1-59253-605-4 (alk. paper)
 ISBN-10: 1-59253-605-0 (alk. paper)
 1. Commercial art--Themes, motives. I. Title. II. Title: Collaborative art journal from the world's most creative graphic designers.
 NC997.V58 2011
 741.6--dc22

                                                        2010031719

 ISBN-13: 978-1-59253-605-4
 ISBN-10: 1-59253-605-0

 10 9 8 7 6 5 4 3 2 1

 Design: James Victore and Chris Thompson

 Printed in China

LUST

A TRAVELING ART JOURNAL
OF GRAPHIC DESIGNERS

Edited by JAMES VICTORE

BEVERLY MASSACHUSETTS

ROCKPORT PUBLISHERS

Contents

What would you do

or make if you had an unlimited budget, a visionary client, and complete control? We all dream of high-paying, high-profile jobs and crave for more creativity in our work. *LUST* is a peek into what is possible when designers are allowed to pursue this dream.

LUST is a collection of unrealized projects and a traveling report of creativity from around the world; a handmade sketchbook zigzagging across six continents, gathering steam, and collecting documents. In it are designers, dreams, and a peek into their processes.

I have selected a list of forty artists, friends, comrades, and collaborators that I have had the great luck to meet over the last twenty-plus years of working and traveling around the globe. Some are newer "young guns," others are design legends—but all share the same passion and love of the profession. This community contains artists from a wide variety of disciplines, including graphic designers, illustrators, type and new media designers, as well as a few anarchists and misfits. Each spent one week with the book and devoted one or two spreads to their "lust," their passion in their own style, in their own voice; sketching, drawing, painting, or collaging directly into the book. When they were finished, the book was passed to the next designer and continent on the list. As it travels around the world it became thicker, packed with art, pregnant with inspirations and ideas.

Dear Jan,

I would like to invite you to contribute to a project of mine called LUST. The premise is this: If, as a designer, you were allowed to follow your bliss and make your dream project—without a budget and freed of client restrictions—what would you do?

Rockport Publishers has given me free rein (and a FedEx account) to send a blank book to all my friends around the world and ask them about their dream jobs, their passions, their LUST. As each designer works directly in the book and passes it forward, it will become progressively fatter and more pregnant with ideas.

I'd love to have you involved. If you are interested in contributing to this project, or need more information, just drop me a line at lust@jamesvictore.com with your contact info and mailing address.

Cheers and best,
James

cultural and political graphics
for the public - on topics as
varied as advertising - human
relations and social issues.
— Victore

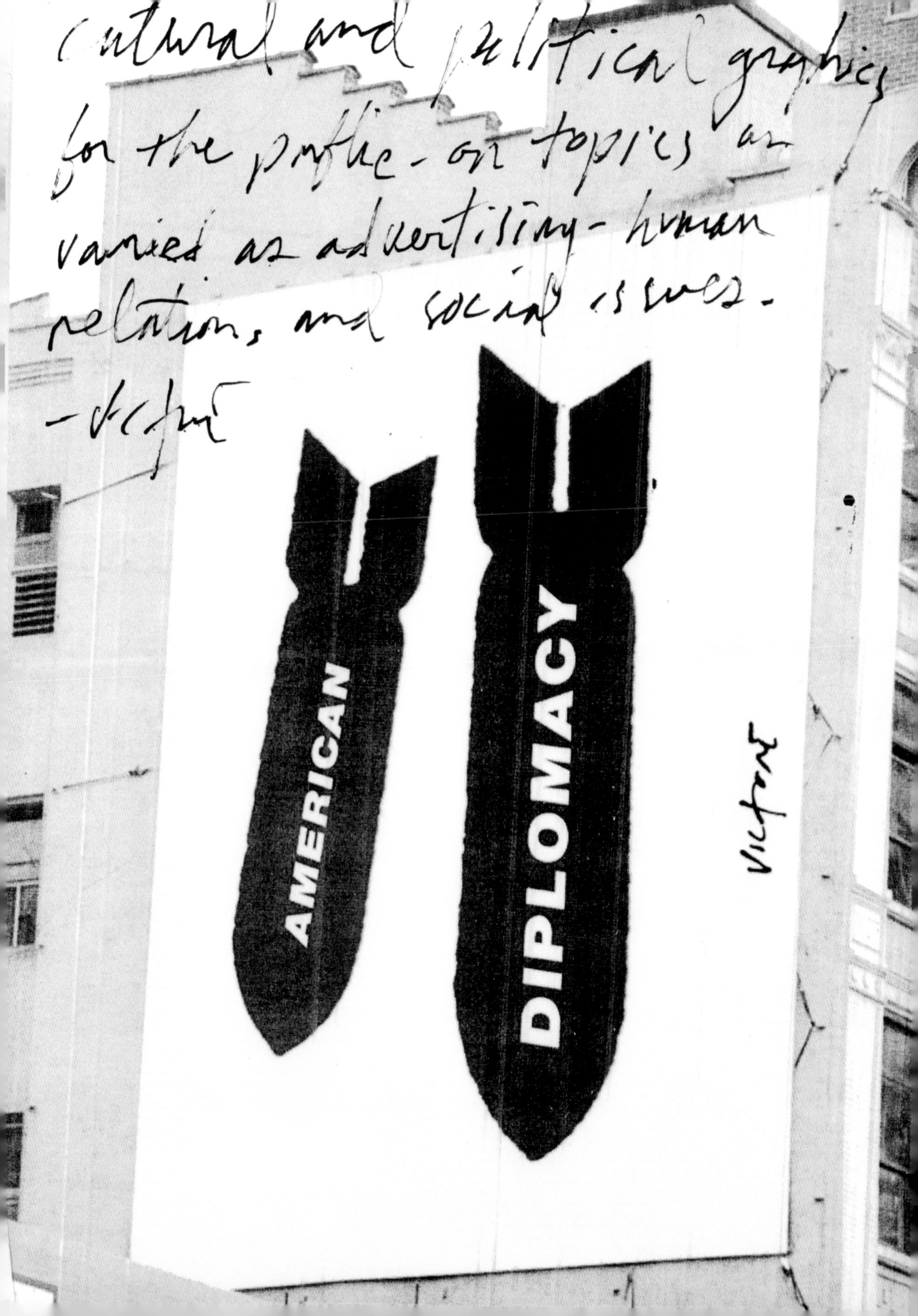

AMERICAN DIPLOMACY

Victore

I dream of finding some
crazy organization or
person who will give me

CHANGE NOW

$50-100-thousand - just to change the world - to be the counter-voice to advertising. I would make social-

I AM THE GEORGE WASHINGTON OF THIS BOOK.

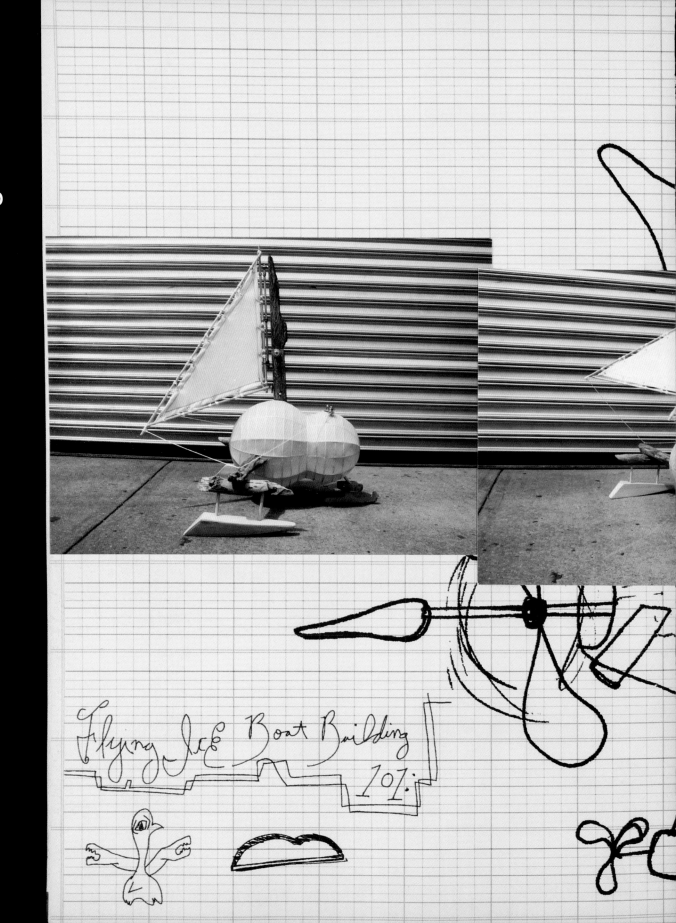

Multi Hull

hinge

fabric
itself
will
keep
taught

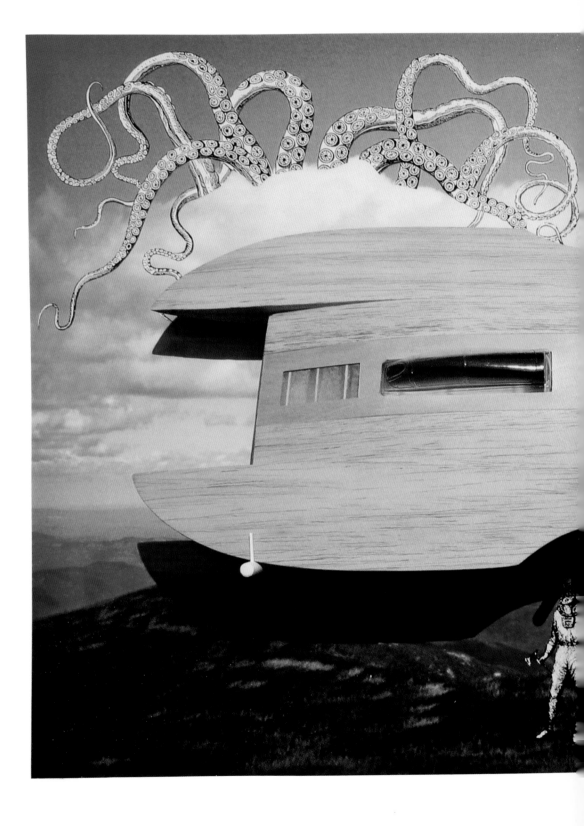

MY LUST IS TO HELP SEPARATE THE TRUTH FROM the TRIVIAL

reak.

ground.

WHO'S GONNA GIVE YOU THAT SOUL TO SOUL
& MAKE YOU WANNA STOW IT IN A GOLDEN
BOWL?

HEAR THAT
CACOPHANY,
old. REEL TO
REEL —
IT'S GONNA
MAKE YOU
MOVE, IT'S
ONNA
MAKE YOU
EEL

LISTEN SCHMISTEN
SEQUINS GLISTEN
DEARTH OF DARING DO?
SENSATE,
~~ESTATE~~, BURN RATE
OLD ~~THINGS~~ ~~REDA-~~   FASCINATE
~~ESCALATES~~

THINK OF SOMETHING
NEW

WHO EVER HEARD OF THAT
SOUND FOR SOUND?
WHO CAN REMEMBER THAT BEAT FO-

MEONE
ME FUN   HIT, HOT, STUPEFACTION.   BEAT
ME
ERTION   ITS   STRANGE, IT'S A CHANGE
AT IS ONE IT'S A NEW REACTION
TODO?

IT'S

AT   TRI - TRIP - TA - TRIP - TA - FI ; FI - TO - FI
         MAYBE TWICE WILL DO.
IT'S.   I ~~KNEW~~ I HAD TO SAY IT, I JUST
HAD
N ONCE DON'T KNOW WHY.
HERE IS THE STUFF WE'RE SUPPOSED TO KNOW?
SCRIBBLED IN A ~~MONUMENT~~ BLOODY GREAT SECRET SHOW.

タイム・マシンがあったら…

大むかしへいって恐竜を見てみたいとか、未来の世界を見てみたいとか、かんがえたことはありませんか？

タイム・マシンがあれば、大むかしや、未来に、かんたんにいけます。

では、タイム・マシンというのは、どういうものなのでしょう？こん週は、時間の世界へごあんないしましょう。

◆構成・少年キング図解班
◆解説・福島正実

え・前村教綱

☆タイム・マシンで、さあ、ゆめの時間旅行に出発だ!!

SF特集 ②

毎日100

★★★★
ウインナチョ
つつみ紙60円
でも結構で

■抽せんて
円盤とふし
をさしあ
■送り先／

■期 間／4
■発 表／

★★★★

神奈川県茅

●テレビ番組

artbr

wonderg

Kyle McDONALD

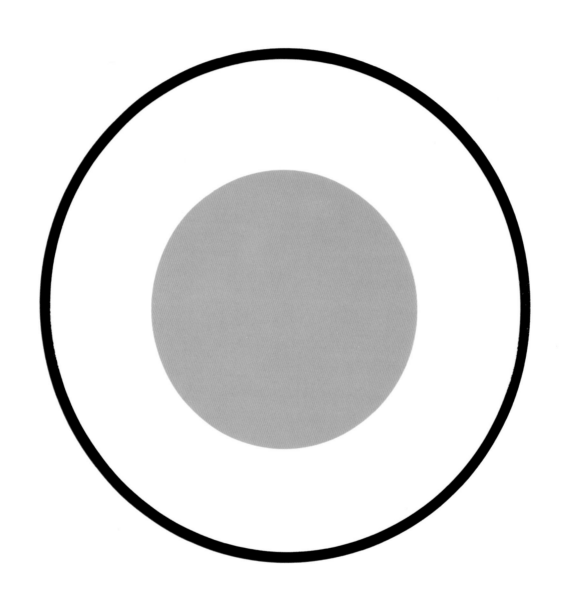

A.

B.

32
Matthias EMSTBERG

RESEARCH AND DEVELOPMENT

http://video2.xtube.com/watch.php?v_user_id=maverickman22&idx=7&v=9dRfX-G630-&cl=ulErt-G630-&from=&ver=3&ccaa=1&qid=&qidx=&qnum=&preview_flag=
http://video2.xtube.com/watch.php?v_user_id=leto3&idx=5&v=6sXh4-G415-&cl=5ElKy-G415-&from=&ver=3&ccaa=1&qid=&qidx=&qnum=&preview_flag=
http://video2.xtube.com/watch.php?v_user_id=Heinz-Bernd&idx=7&v=PbgHt-G517-&cl=sCKtr-G517-&from=&ver=3&ccaa=1&qid=&qidx=&qnum=&preview_flag=
http://video2.xtube.com/watch.php?v_user_id=jordanross&idx=5&v=21oro-C218-&cl=1b8bm-C218-&from=&ver=3&ccaa=1&qid=&qidx=&qnum=&preview_flag=
http://video2.xtube.com/watch.php?v_user_id=sam1475&idx=1&v=99IBRy1XPBf&cl=esSmN6d13cr&from=&ver=3&ccaa=1&qid=&qidx=&qnum=&preview_flag=
http://video2.xtube.com/watch.php?v_user_id=bhudagod81&idx=8&v=UeZci_S626_&cl=sS0cA_S626_&from=&ver=3&ccaa=1&qid=&qidx=&qnum=&preview_flag=
http://video2.xtube.com/watch.php?v_user_id=welhorny&idx=8&v=R4CGL_G628_&cl=SkKfv_G628_&from=&ver=3&ccaa=1&qid=&qidx=&qnum=&preview_flag=
http://video2.xtube.com/watch.php?v_user_id=btownguy20&idx=7&v=QZWVZ-G527-&cl=2aiS5-G527-&from=&ver=3&ccaa=1&qid=&qidx=&qnum=&preview_flag=
http://video2.xtube.com/watch.php?v_user_id=hotboycamz&idx=8&v=1Fb9n_C521_&cl=CjLS7_C521_&from=&ver=3&ccaa=1&qid=&qidx=&qnum=&preview_flag=
http://video2.xtube.com/watch.php?v_user_id=knotaboyscout&idx=8&v=DZOrT_G622_&cl=6zvdU_G622_&from=&ver=3&ccaa=1&qid=&qidx=&qnum=&preview_flag=
http://video2.xtube.com/watch.php?v_user_id=lovemonkeywa&idx=6&v=chBRI_G227_&cl=F3wjF_G227_&from=&ver=3&ccaa=1&qid=&qidx=&qnum=&preview_flag=
http://video2.xtube.com/watch.php?v_user_id=uhohbentover&idx=2&v=99AqUlFuvLn&cl=jTGKowFfePU&from=&ver=3&ccaa=1&qid=&qidx=&qnum=&preview_flag=
http://video2.xtube.com/watch.php?v_user_id=hotboycamz&idx=5&v=gUQa2-G129-&cl=R2U2y-G129-&from=&ver=3&ccaa=1&qid=&qidx=&qnum=&preview_flag=
http://video2.xtube.com/watch.php?v_user_id=nybetty&idx=7&v=QCtHh-G622-&cl=37AY3-G622-&from=&ver=3&ccaa=1&qid=&qidx=&qnum=&preview_flag=
http://video2.xtube.com/watch.php?v_user_id=billyvacation&idx=6&v=4X8yZ_G221_&cl=g8Qb9_G221_&from=&ver=3&ccaa=1&qid=&qidx=&qnum=&preview_flag=
http://video2.xtube.com/watch.php?v_user_id=cacau123&idx=5&v=n3n8o-G416-&cl=mE1IT-G416-&from=&ver=3&ccaa=1&qid=&qidx=&qnum=&preview_flag=
http://video2.xtube.com/watch.php?v_user_id=hotbtmfcktoy&idx=8&v=719Mo_G816_&cl=vPv70_G816_&from=&ver=3&ccaa=1&qid=&qidx=&qnum=&preview_flag=
http://video2.xtube.com/watch.php?v_user_id=TheSecondFirst&idx=7&v=iPw0C-G820-&cl=tAhpG-G820-&from=&ver=3&ccaa=1&qid=&qidx=&qnum=&preview_flag=
http://video2.xtube.com/watch.php?v_user_id=nostradamus&idx=5&v=3jMEE-C415-&cl=FbAKk-C415-&from=&ver=3&ccaa=1&qid=&qidx=&qnum=&preview_flag=
http://video2.xtube.com/watch.php?v_user_id=urban04&idx=5&v=XtGME-C422-&cl=FXAwc-C422-&from=&ver=3&ccaa=1&qid=&qidx=&qnum=&preview_flag=
http://video2.xtube.com/watch.php?v_user_id=urban04&idx=6&v=BkAPQ_C322_&cl=WJJ3x_C322_&from=&ver=3&ccaa=1&qid=&qidx=&qnum=&preview_flag=
http://video2.xtube.com/watch.php?v_user_id=SE6SEX&idx=6&v=YPe4e_S416_&cl=YL9fa_S416_&from=&ver=3&ccaa=1&qid=&qidx=&qnum=&preview_flag=
http://video2.xtube.com/watch.php?v_user_id=anthonycefala&idx=2&v=98x1kXF5oc6&cl=nIZmA9VJeRR&from=&ver=3&ccaa=1&qid=&qidx=&qnum=&preview_flag=
http://video2.xtube.com/watch.php?v_user_id=gymtrat69&idx=7&v=1fWWa-G529-&cl=2yJov-G529-&from=&ver=3&ccaa=1&qid=&qidx=&qnum=&preview_flag=
http://video2.xtube.com/watch.php?v_user_id=gymtrat69&idx=5&v=cNozP-G421-&cl=cbxq2-G421-&from=&ver=3&ccaa=1&qid=&qidx=&qnum=&preview_flag=
http://video2.xtube.com/watch.php?v_user_id=jo420&idx=3&v=99IsoRGtHVu&cl=XQncrxgzTTC&from=&ver=3&ccaa=1&qid=&qidx=&qnum=&preview_flag=
http://video2.xtube.com/watch.php?v_user_id=jo420&idx=3&v=99tpQ3UchU1&cl=WYBkzNxPdWk&from=&ver=3&ccaa=1&qid=&qidx=&qnum=&preview_flag=
http://video2.xtube.com/watch.php?v_user_id=silver1078&idx=8&v=ek6kR_G716_&cl=KmJBm_G716_&from=&ver=3&ccaa=1&qid=&qidx=&qnum=&preview_flag=
http://video2.xtube.com/watch.php?v_user_id=silver1078&idx=8&v=QQyCm_G518_&cl=51V5n_G518_&from=&ver=3&ccaa=1&qid=&qidx=&qnum=&preview_flag=
http://video2.xtube.com/watch.php?v_user_id=jockzzz&idx=6&v=TJMv4Qm811_&cl=y4RzneWimu_&from=&ver=3&ccaa=1&qid=&qidx=&qnum=&preview_flag=
http://video2.xtube.com/watch.php?v_user_id=roverri40&idx=7&v=rpDgM-C827-&cl=bMpGp-C827-&from=&ver=3&ccaa=1&qid=&qidx=&qnum=&preview_flag=
http://video2.xtube.com/watch.php?v_user_id=glandjuteux&idx=8&v=nr7vL_C514_&cl=MLntf_C514_&from=&ver=3&ccaa=1&qid=&qidx=&qnum=&preview_flag=
http://video2.xtube.com/watch.php?v_user_id=dude_hu&idx=7&v=MRQAz-G825-&cl=0QpoL-G825-&from=&ver=3&ccaa=1&qid=&qidx=&qnum=&preview_flag=
http://video2.xtube.com/watch.php?v_user_id=dude_hu&idx=6&v=fpk7x_C424_&cl=7grfj_C424_&from=&ver=3&ccaa=1&qid=&qidx=&qnum=&preview_flag=
http://video2.xtube.com/watch.php?v_user_id=tadna&idx=8&v=ztas0_G816_&cl=G8flP_G816_&from=&ver=3&ccaa=1&qid=&qidx=&qnum=&preview_flag=
http://video2.xtube.com/watch.php?v_user_id=solodude&idx=6&v=gTvaT_J124_&cl=dQGGv_J124_&from=&ver=3&ccaa=1&qid=&qidx=&qnum=&preview_flag=
http://video2.xtube.com/watch.php?v_user_id=homosuckiens&idx=5&v=pTeJ19Y610-&cl=X1BAplLdZ3-&from=&ver=3&ccaa=1&qid=&qidx=&qnum=&preview_flag=
http://video2.xtube.com/watch.php?v_user_id=oneeyedjap&idx=5&v=lyyl1-G427-&cl=09p1s-G427-&from=&ver=3&ccaa=1&qid=&qidx=&qnum=&preview_flag=
http://video2.xtube.com/watch.php?v_user_id=SukkOnThis&idx=7&v=9unMi-C520-&cl=f7GSH-C520-&from=&ver=3&ccaa=1&qid=&qidx=&qnum=&preview_flag=
http://video2.xtube.com/watch.php?v_user_id=MikeyFromGeorgia&idx=4&v=99jSfXLXMZC&cl=mDoNrtervJw&from=&ver=3&ccaa=1&qid=&qidx=&qnum=&preview_flag=
http://video2.xtube.com/watch.php?v_user_id=GoliathDave&idx=7&v=gU7wy-G715-&cl=6jth4-G715-&from=&ver=3&ccaa=1&qid=&qidx=&qnum=&preview_flag=
http://video2.xtube.com/watch.php?v_user_id=bostonbigred&idx=2&v=99U4uf57xFK&cl=jE7fcfyPRKQ&from=&ver=3&ccaa=1&qid=&qidx=&qnum=&preview_flag=
http://video2.xtube.com/watch.php?v_user_id=GoliathDave&idx=2&v=99LYODmVBoX&cl=lavLRoR91RX&from=&ver=3&ccaa=1&qid=&qidx=&qnum=&preview_flag=
http://video2.xtube.com/watch.php?v_user_id=hotgaynerdsf&idx=4&v=99grOAFIVP5&cl=xfGu8SvgP2A&from=&ver=3&ccaa=1&qid=&qidx=&qnum=&preview_flag=
http://video2.xtube.com/watch.php?v_user_id=hotgaynerdsf&idx=8&v=HraidiK013_&cl=2U9D1seQDX_&from=&ver=3&ccaa=1&qid=&qidx=&qnum=&preview_flag=
http://video2.xtube.com/watch.php?v_user_id=DyrtyD&idx=8&v=OPPSL_G717_&cl=zRsbu_G717_&from=&ver=3&ccaa=1&qid=&qidx=&qnum=&preview_flag=
http://video2.xtube.com/watch.php?v_user_id=marcelbln&idx=7&v=r7Fsc-G729-&cl=Dpv1T-G729-&from=&ver=3&ccaa=1&qid=&qidx=&qnum=&preview_flag=
http://video2.xtube.com/watch.php?v_user_id=grobes_geraet&idx=6&v=KnytH_G330_&cl=PcBrT_G330_&from=&ver=3&ccaa=1&qid=&qidx=&qnum=&preview_flag=
http://video2.xtube.com/watch.php?v_user_id=grobes_geraet&idx=8&v=zens2_G829_&cl=rS44S_G829_&from=&ver=3&ccaa=1&qid=&qidx=&qnum=&preview_flag=
http://video2.xtube.com/watch.php?v_user_id=SpunkWorthy_dotCom&idx=5&v=6ppPh-C328-&cl=aAAi3-C328-&from=&ver=3&ccaa=1&qid=&qidx=&qnum=&preview_flag=
http://video2.xtube.com/watch.php?v_user_id=maverickman22&idx=6&v=HioH3_G129_&cl=JUKo8_G129_&from=&ver=3&ccaa=1&qid=&qidx=&qnum=&preview_flag=
http://video2.xtube.com/watch.php?v_user_id=maverickman22&idx=6&v=HioH3_G129_&cl=JUKo8_G129_&from=&ver=3&ccaa=1&qid=&qidx=&qnum=&preview_flag=
http://video2.xtube.com/watch.php?v_user_id=lyrique&idx=8&v=YlREw_C617_&cl=0Hdkc_C617_&from=&ver=3&ccaa=1&qid=&qidx=&qnum=&preview_flag=
http://video2.xtube.com/watch.php?v_user_id=lyrique&idx=7&v=3IJiY-C517-&cl=Tuq94-C517-&from=&ver=3&ccaa=1&qid=&qidx=&qnum=&preview_flag=
http://video2.xtube.com/watch.php?v_user_id=hardchivo&idx=8&v=ArVhr_G529_&cl=CPmuh_G529_&from=&ver=3&ccaa=1&qid=&qidx=&qnum=&preview_flag=
http://video2.xtube.com/watch.php?v_user_id=TommyTank86&idx=6&v=SWLG4_G419_&cl=BMxbp_G419_&from=&ver=3&ccaa=1&qid=&qidx=&qnum=&preview_flag=
http://video2.xtube.com/watch.php?v_user_id=mynameisjake00&idx=8&v=UyfEA_J822_&cl=XejiF_J822_&from=&ver=3&ccaa=1&qid=&qidx=&qnum=&preview_flag=
http://video2.xtube.com/watch.php?v_user_id=thetox&idx=3&v=1AipCpsYw5V&cl=c5twOFDBzms&from=&ver=3&ccaa=1&qid=&qidx=&qnum=&preview_flag=
http://video2.xtube.com/watch.php?v_user_id=WhoWMan&idx=8&v=xOKxO_C818_&cl=XLwbd_C818_&from=&ver=3&ccaa=1&qid=&qidx=&qnum=&preview_flag=
http://video2.xtube.com/watch.php?v_user_id=stixis&idx=7&v=CjyghCp512-&cl=rfO9JXMkwF-&from=&ver=3&ccaa=1&qid=&qidx=&qnum=&preview_flag=
http://video2.xtube.com/watch.php?v_user_id=atlmodelguy&idx=1&v=99ecPFY8wLz&cl=EFuAc1t7Xa3&from=&ver=3&ccaa=1&qid=&qidx=&qnum=&preview_flag=
http://video2.xtube.com/watch.php?v_user_id=Troofire&idx=7&v=cE6z4-G721-&cl=9Lsnj-G721-&from=&ver=3&ccaa=1&qid=&qidx=&qnum=&preview_flag=
http://video2.xtube.com/watch.php?v_user_id=middleguys&idx=6&v=ylQgH_G221_&cl=MQ3V1_G221_&from=&ver=3&ccaa=1&qid=&qidx=&qnum=&preview_flag=
http://video2.xtube.com/watch.php?v_user_id=2Gingercocks&idx=8&v=7bn3Z_G826_&cl=7Y02U_G826_&from=&ver=3&ccaa=1&qid=&qidx=&qnum=&preview_flag=
http://video2.xtube.com/watch.php?v_user_id=hairyalaskanartist&idx=6&v=dswQQ_G116_&cl=Vupta_G116_&from=&ver=3&ccaa=1&qid=&qidx=&qnum=&preview_flag=
http://video2.xtube.com/watch.php?v_user_id=rigormorning&idx=7&v=16Qz4JB911-&cl=3BpBlkEyHm-&from=&ver=3&ccaa=1&qid=&qidx=&qnum=&preview_flag=
http://video2.xtube.com/watch.php?v_user_id=Do_Me_Bare&idx=8&v=Hbx5g_G724_&cl=iUiEY_G724_&from=&ver=3&ccaa=1&qid=&qidx=&qnum=&preview_flag=
http://video2.xtube.com/watch_video.php?v_user_id=drachon222&idx=8&v=K07mb_J820_&cl=2iWTF_J820_&from=&ver=3&ccaa=1&qid=&qidx=&qnum=&preview_flag=
http://video2.xtube.com/watch_video.php?v_user_id=KlappenSexBerlin&idx=8&v=TC7QM_G626_&cl=DhvBi_G626_&from=&ver=3&ccaa=1&qid=&qidx=&qnum=&preview_flag=
http://video2.xtube.com/watch_video.php?v_user_id=jonathanmasoch&idx=5&v=ypZFXrA509-&cl=5q6UTs1ShG-&from=&ver=3&ccaa=1&qid=&qidx=&qnum=&preview_flag=
http://video2.xtube.com/watch_video.php?v_user_id=jock-spank&idx=5&v=mW8mz-G214-&cl=TZd9e-G214-&from=&ver=3&ccaa=1&qid=&qidx=&qnum=&preview_flag=
http://video2.xtube.com/watch.php?v_user_id=ypofero&idx=8&v=VARu3_G717_&cl=Prkqg_G717_&from=&ver=3&ccaa=1&qid=&qidx=&qnum=&preview_flag=
http://video2.xtube.com/watch_video.php?v_user_id=ctrxxx&idx=8&v=ACPYhVM809_&cl=CboiDEcfSR_&from=&ver=3&ccaa=1&qid=&qidx=&qnum=&preview_flag=
http://video2.xtube.com/watch_video.php?v_user_id=ctrxxx&idx=8&v=ACPYhVM809_&cl=CboiDEcfSR_&from=&ver=3&ccaa=1&qid=&qidx=&qnum=&preview_flag=
http://video2.xtube.com/watch.php?v_user_id=smokingpole&idx=2&v=99v99f0T8QQ&cl=lNU9HjhKc0W&from=&ver=3&ccaa=1&qid=&qidx=&qnum=&preview_flag
http://video2.xtube.com/watch.php?v_user_id=jahinky80&idx=8&v=dNCyPQu312_&cl=lO2XuzO9P9_&from=&ver=3&ccaa=1&qid=&qidx=&qnum=&preview_flag=
http://video2.xtube.com/watch.php?v_user_id=trev420&idx=8&v=IxHfIjC813_&cl=dwY5q_C813_&from=&ver=3&ccaa=1&qid=&qidx=&qnum=&preview_flag=
http://video2.xtube.com/watch.php?v_user_id=garwolfnyc&idx=1&v=98f8GgDc2uy&cl=96SBJYYwyt6&from=&ver=3&ccaa=1&qid=&qidx=&qnum=&preview_flag=
http://video2.xtube.com/watch.php?v_user_id=toddfun&idx=7&v=1IFdX-G528-&cl=cWz3C-G528-&from=&ver=3&ccaa=1&qid=&qidx=&qnum=&preview_flag=
http://video2.xtube.com/watch.php?v_user_id=zivgr25&idx=7&v=diGrOBD009-&cl=CHQR3riTfe-&from=&ver=3&ccaa=1&qid=&qidx=&qnum=&preview_flag=
http://video2.xtube.com/watch.php?v_user_id=spurtnow&idx=6&v=QzqBNXG313_&cl=QQj6V_G313_&from=&ver=3&ccaa=1&qid=&qidx=&qnum=&preview_flag=
http://video2.xtube.com/watch.php?v_user_id=xmil2007&idx=6&v=MpaOk_C317_&cl=V2UuD_C317_&from=&ver=3&ccaa=1&qid=&qidx=&qnum=&preview_flag=
http://video2.xtube.com/watch.php?v_user_id=xmil2007&idx=6&v=ZlvuS_G317_&cl=JRkFo_G317_&from=&ver=3&ccaa=1&qid=&qidx=&qnum=&preview_flag=
http://video2.xtube.com/watch.php?v_user_id=maverickman22&idx=6&v=7rdpu_G323_&cl=0eR9D_G323_&from=&ver=3&ccaa=1&qid=&qidx=&qnum=&preview_flag=
http://video2.xtube.com/watch.php?v_user_id=irishmuscle71&idx=5&v=5Xeik-G416-&cl=6Cvep-G416-&from=&ver=3&ccaa=1&qid=&qidx=&qnum=&preview_flag=
http://video2.xtube.com/watch.php?v_user_id=hotgaynerdsf&idx=1&v=99U3liFvEmt&cl=nwhLZzw1TR2&from=&ver=3&ccaa=1&qid=&qidx=&qnum=&preview_flag=
http://video2.xtube.com/watch.php?v_user_id=Rockstars721&idx=8&v=JLltV_G520_&cl=gm2Tm_G520_&from=&ver=3&ccaa=1&qid=&qidx=&qnum=&preview_flag=

http://video2.xtube.com/watch.php?v_user_id=Rockstars721&idx=8&v=9FpDb_G830_&cl=tS2WQ_G830_&from=&ver=3&ccaa=1&qid=&qidx=&qnum=&preview_flag=
http://video2.xtube.com/watch.php?v_user_id=Rockstars721&idx=7&v=9pKkj-G529-&cl=qOSic-G529-&from=&ver=3&ccaa=1&qid=&qidx=&qnum=&preview_flag=
http://video2.xtube.com/watch.php?v_user_id=gay05&idx=7&v=j2bHc-G527_&cl=Q4ps8-G527-&from=&ver=3&ccaa=1&qid=&qidx=&qnum=&preview_flag=
http://video2.xtube.com/watch.php?v_user_id=hotbttmfcktoy&idx=8&v=KDP3r_C816_&cl=Nm43x_C816_&from=&ver=3&ccaa=1&qid=&qidx=&qnum=&preview_flag=
http://video2.xtube.com/watch.php?v_user_id=Bubblefist&idx=6&v=NCpnY_G323_&cl=ijasG_G323_&from=&ver=3&ccaa=1&qid=&qidx=&qnum=&preview_flag=
http://video2.xtube.com/watch.php?v_user_id=Tyd23133&idx=8&v=3lW2B_G822_&cl=kViTt_G822_&from=&ver=3&ccaa=1&qid=&qidx=&qnum=&preview_flag=
http://video2.xtube.com/watch.php?v_user_id=pumaguy80&idx=8&v=4T4AP_G616_&cl=g6nlE_G616_&from=&ver=3&ccaa=1&qid=&qidx=&qnum=&preview_flag=
http://video2.xtube.com/watch.php?v_user_id=xraydanny&idx=7&v=VyLru-G718_&cl=Es6wW-G718-&from=&ver=3&ccaa=1&qid=&qidx=&qnum=&preview_flag=
http://video2.xtube.com/watch.php?v_user_id=garwolfnyc&idx=5&v=qpO4HnC111-&cl=8IGGyzgo5x-&from=&ver=3&ccaa=1&qid=&qidx=&qnum=&preview_flag=
http://video2.xtube.com/watch.php?v_user_id=bighorndog&idx=1&v=992ON906rY1&cl=E5hT8JYehjw&from=&ver=3&ccaa=1&qid=&qidx=&qnum=&preview_flag=
http://video2.xtube.com/watch.php?v_user_id=bumbers&idx=6&v=Vr7Eh_G215_&cl=OPg6U_G215_&from=&ver=3&ccaa=1&qid=&qidx=&qnum=&preview_flag=
http://video2.xtube.com/watch.php?v_user_id=ozrockster&idx=6&v=61cno_G319_&cl=e2tzh_G319_&from=&ver=3&ccaa=1&qid=&qidx=&qnum=&preview_flag=
http://video2.xtube.com/watch.php?v_user_id=MontanaFever8x7&idx=7&v=zbpYFm8111-&cl=e2szQOdie3-&from=&ver=3&ccaa=1&qid=&qidx=&qnum=&preview_flag=
http://video2.xtube.com/watch.php?v_user_id=sethmiller1980&idx=6&v=cMy61_G424_&cl=LfSqg_G424_&from=&ver=3&ccaa=1&qid=&qidx=&qnum=&preview_flag=
http://video2.xtube.com/watch.php?v_user_id=sethmiller1980&idx=6&v=XQJ5S_G127_&cl=vmpYT_G127_&from=&ver=3&ccaa=1&qid=&qidx=&qnum=&preview_flag=
http://video2.xtube.com/watch.php?v_user_id=hotboycamz&idx=7&v=VfkdE-C618_&cl=UAPZj-C618-&from=&ver=3&ccaa=1&qid=&qidx=&qnum=&preview_flag=
http://video2.xtube.com/watch.php?v_user_id=hotboycamz&idx=8&v=LBVKd_G829_&cl=Fal.Hu_G829_&from=&ver=3&ccaa=1&qid=&qidx=&qnum=&preview_flag=
http://video2.xtube.com/watch.php?v_user_id=hotnaco&idx=8&v=A1cql_S829_&cl=txW2p_S829_&from=&ver=3&ccaa=1&qid=&qidx=&qnum=&preview_flag=
http://video2.xtube.com/watch.php?v_user_id=hotnaco&idx=8&v=A1cql_S829_&cl=txW2p_S829_&from=&ver=3&ccaa=1&qid=&qidx=&qnum=&preview_flag=
http://video2.xtube.com/watch.php?v_user_id=hornosuckiens&idx=5&v=pTeJ19Y610-&cl=X1BAplLdZ3-&from=&ver=3&ccaa=1&qid=&qidx=&qnum=&preview_flag=
http://video2.xtube.com/watch.php?v_user_id=hairyalaskanartist&idx=6&v=dswQQ_G116_&cl=Vupta_G116_&from=&ver=3&ccaa=1&qid=&qidx=&qnum=&preview_flag=
http://video2.xtube.com/watch.php?v_user_id=hotwariner&idx=7&v=BA0I4g0412-&cl=nZANey7grr-&from=&ver=3&ccaa=1&qid=&qidx=&qnum=&preview_flag=
http://video2.xtube.com/watch.php?v_user_id=hotwariner&idx=8&v=pQt0f_G529_&cl=LaAuO_G529_&from=&ver=3&ccaa=1&qid=&qidx=&qnum=&preview_flag=
http://video2.xtube.com/watch.php?v_user_id=bumbers&idx=6&v=Vr7Eh_G215_&cl=OPg6U_G215_&from=&ver=3&ccaa=1&qid=&qidx=&qnum=&preview_flag=

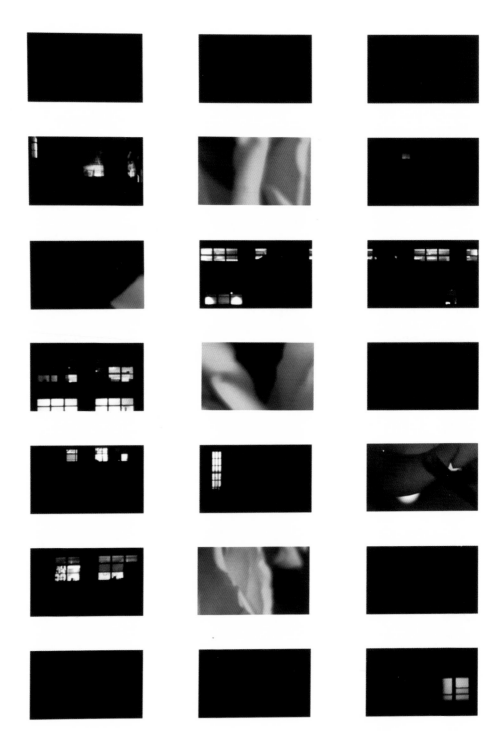

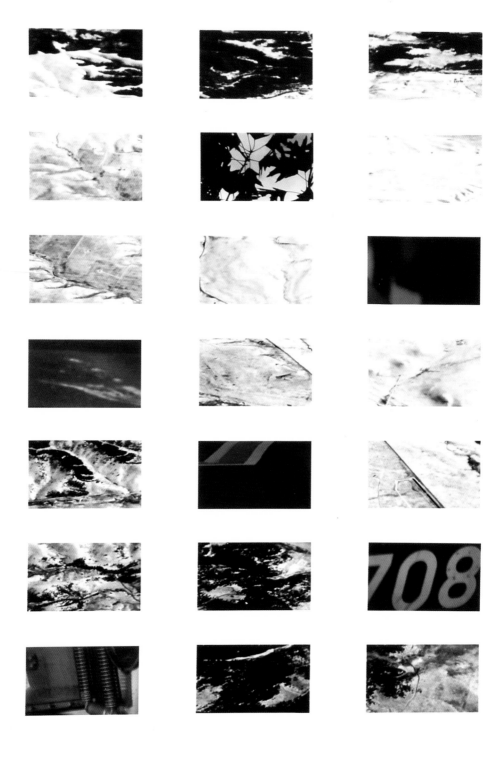

THE USE OF ANIMALS

DENTIST

S. CHWAST

Chaz MAVIYANE-DAVIES

The Book of
ASSERTIONS
VERSE 45

The Book of
ASSERTIONS

VERSE 27

MANTONE®
NATIVE AMERICAN

MANTONE®
HISPANIC AMERICAN

MANTONE®
AFRICAN AMERICAN

MANTONE®
ASIAN AMERICAN

MANTONE®
AMERICAN ?

The Book of
ASSERTIONS

VERSE 31

IF SOMEBODY GAVE ME $1,000,000., I'D CREATE 2 SHIPPING CONTAINER

DESIGNERS WOULD CUSTOMIZE THEIR CONTAINER

VILLAGES WHERE YOUNG DESIGNERS COULD LIVE/WORK AND DO PROJECTS FOR THE GREATER GOOD.

PROJECT M
VILLAGE NORTH
BELFAST, ME

DESIGNERS COULD MIGRATE BACK & FORTH.

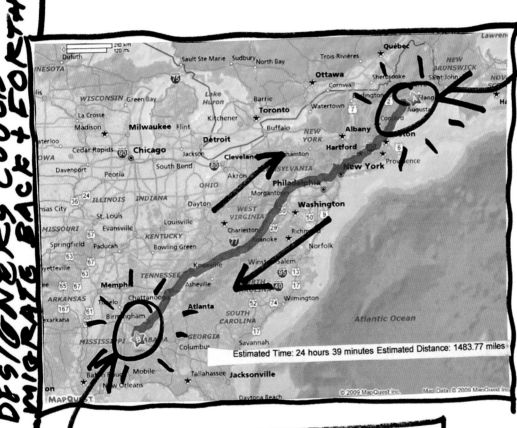

Estimated Time: 24 hours 39 minutes Estimated Distance: 1483.77 miles

PROJECT M
VILLAGE SOUTH
GREENSBORO, AL

Lanny SOMMESE

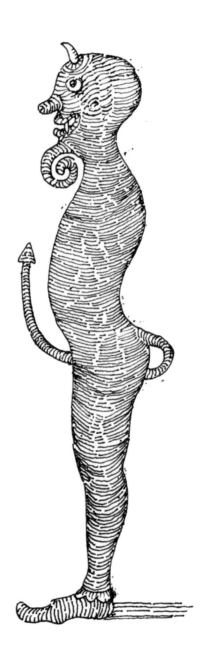

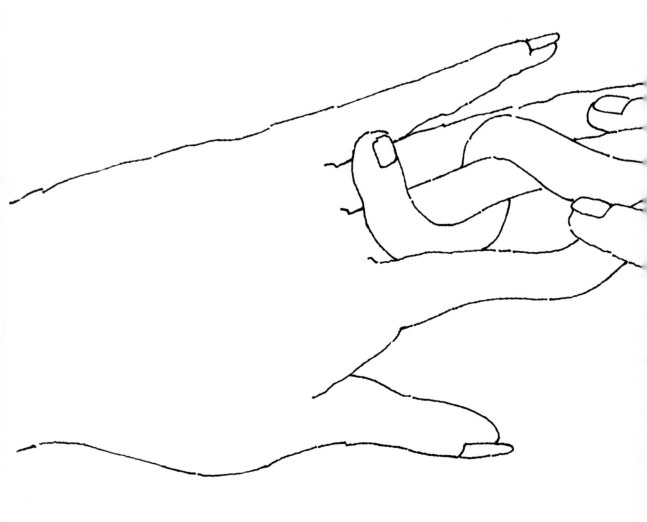

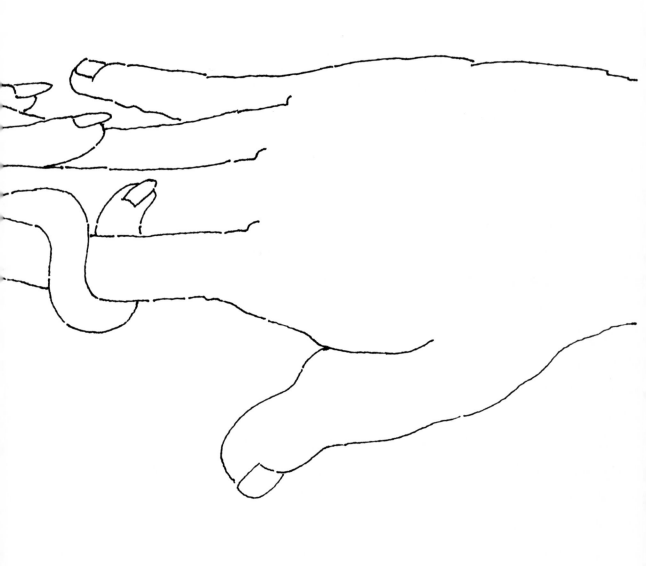

Matthew McGUINNESS

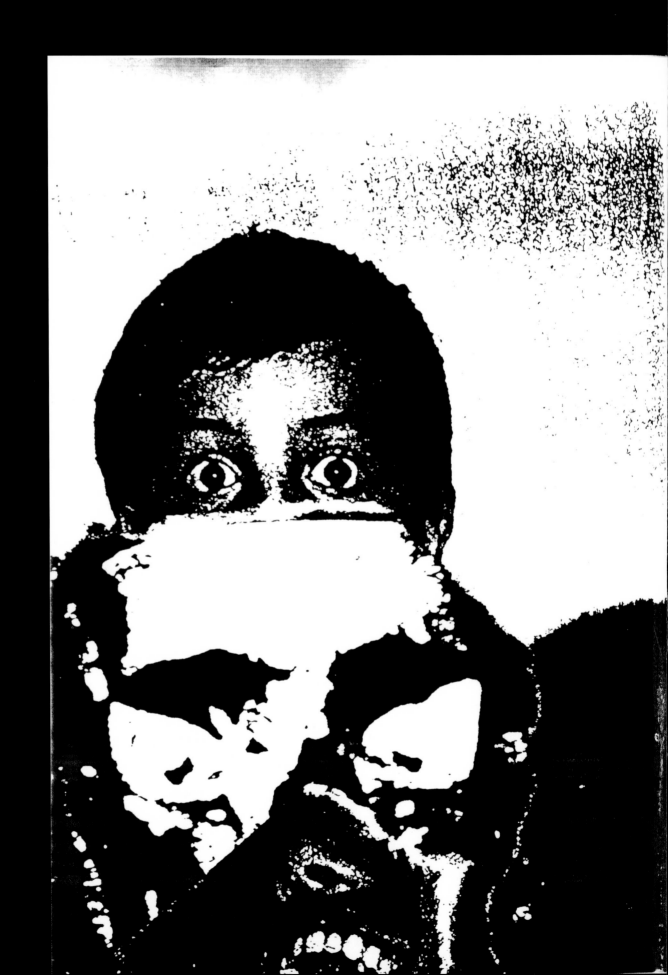

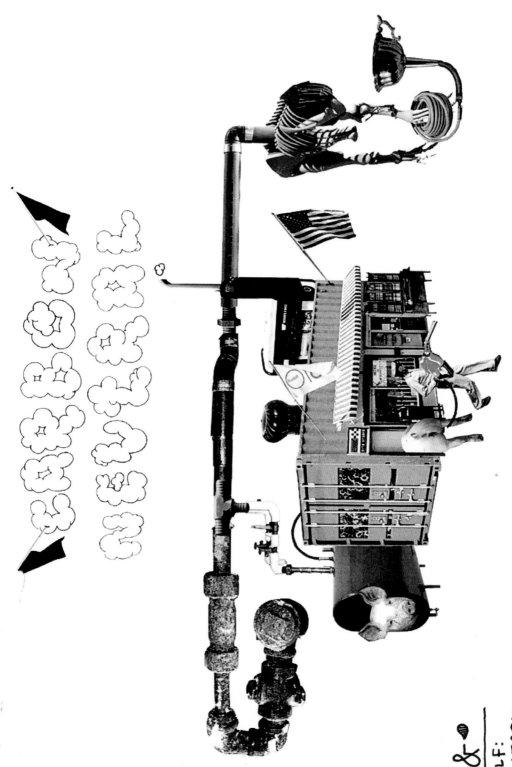

RUDOLF:
A SALUTARY
PIPELINE *

Female cyclist hit by lorry in Peckham High Street

Woman seriously injured after being hit by a lorry while cycling in Peckham High Street during rush-hour traffic

by: Rhodri Phillips

2 June 2009

Scene w... ...was hit by a lorry on Peckham High Street

The woman +whos name+ +I can not+ +find+ lived

* _____ *

many others HAVE NOT BEEN SO LUCKY

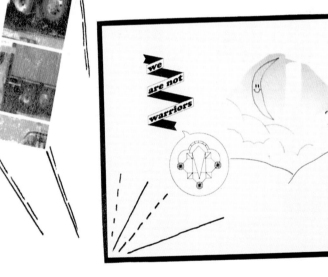

we are not warriors

AS MORE CYCLISTS BEGIN TO SHOW PLEASE ALLOW THEM. *Nurture* & *to Grow*

BLACK & WHITE
_____

→ WHEN ONE GOES OFF TO PLAY TENNIS OR FOOTBALL THE RISK OF DEATH IS NEXT TO NILL BUT GO FOR A BIKE RIDE!!! WEE!!! WEEE REAL Horror Show

BUMS RIDE FREE Extirior might by way of brush

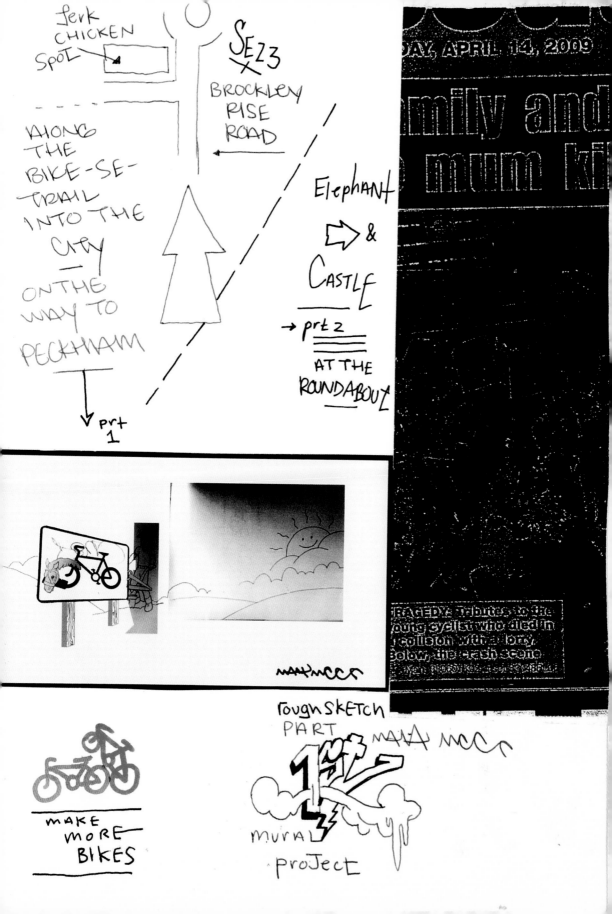

Jerk CHICKEN SPOT

SE23
BROCKLEY RISE ROAD

ALONG THE BIKE-SE-TRAIL INTO THE CITY — ONTHE WAY TO PECKHAM

prt 1

Elephant ⇒ & CASTLE

→ prt 2

AT THE ROUNDABOUT

DAY, APRIL 14, 2009

mily and mum ki

TRAGEDY: Tributes to the young cyclist who died in a collision with a lorry. Below, the crash scene

rough SKETCH PART

MAKE MORE BIKES

1ST

MURAL PROJECT

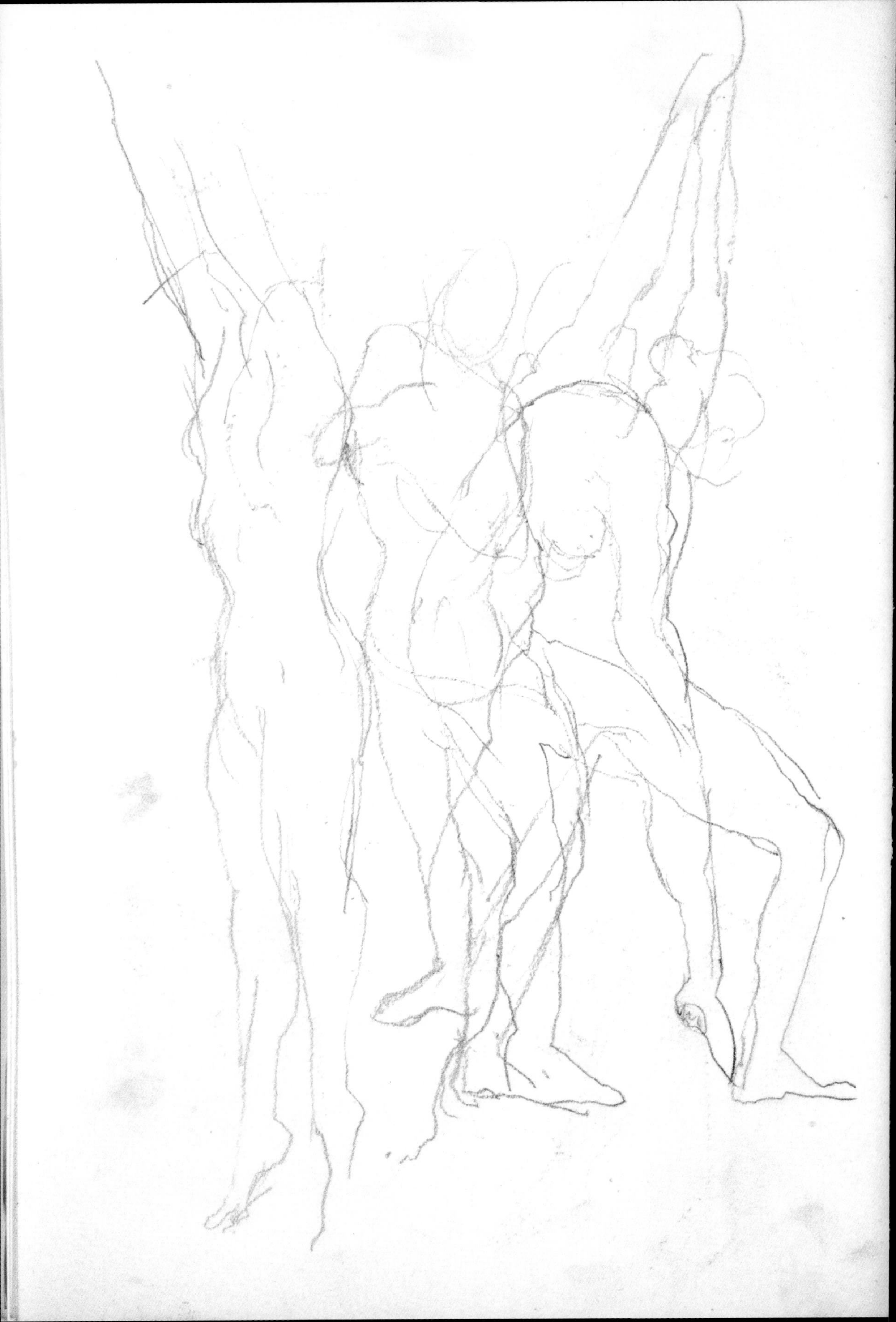

WilFierborn 2009

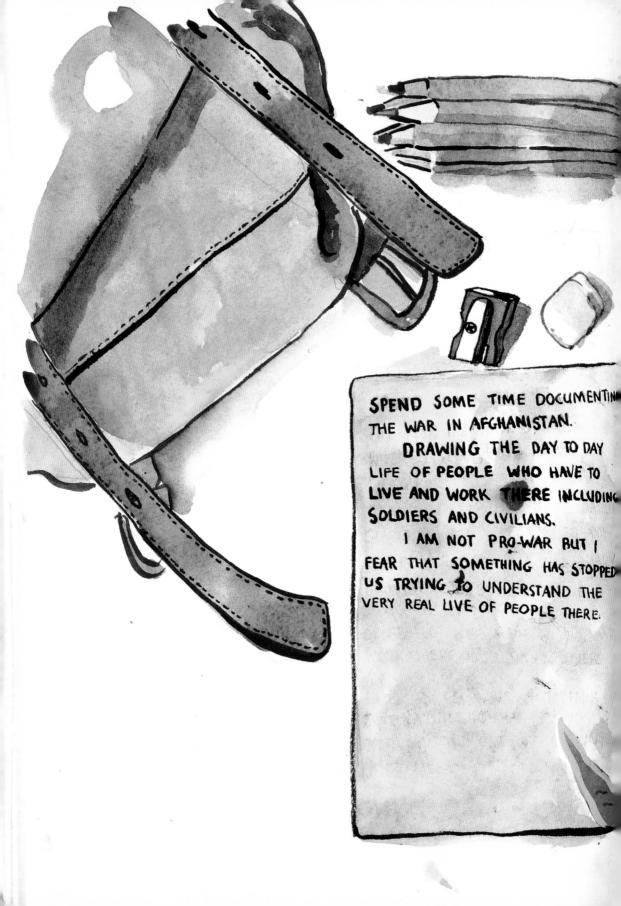

SPEND SOME TIME DOCUMENTIN
THE WAR IN AFGHANISTAN.
DRAWING THE DAY TO DAY
LIFE OF PEOPLE WHO HAVE TO
LIVE AND WORK THERE INCLUDING
SOLDIERS AND CIVILIANS.
I AM NOT PRO-WAR BUT I
FEAR THAT SOMETHING HAS STOPPED
US TRYING TO UNDERSTAND THE
VERY REAL LIVE OF PEOPLE THERE.

AFGHANISTAN

WILFREEBORN '09

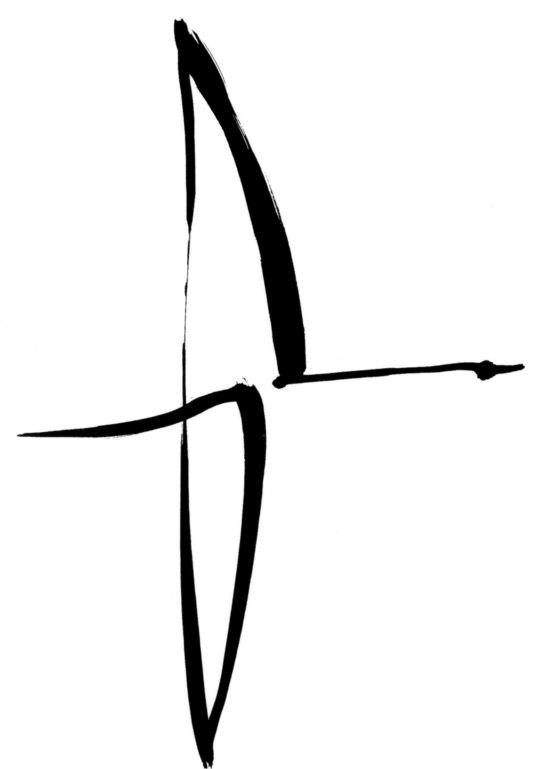

Kari Piippo

Kari Piippo

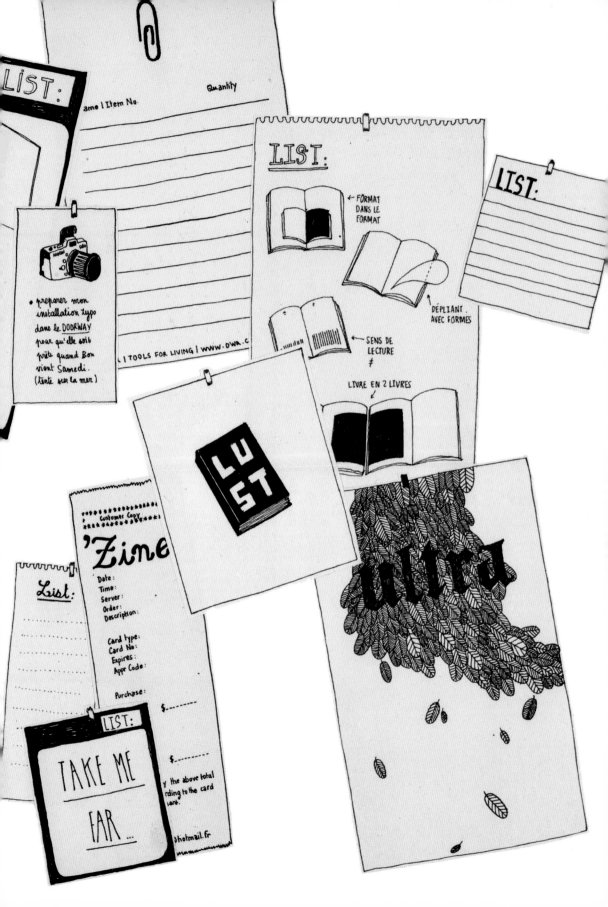

List:

Dentelles?

**Work hard,
play harder**
...

Thanks James

THE
LOST
BOOK

NOT FOR SALE...

THE NOTEBOOK PROJECT:

PUT YOUR NOTEBOOK IN A
LIBRARY OR BOOKSTORE
WITH YOUR NAME AND EMAIL
ADRESS AND SEE WHAT
HAPPENS.

IT HAS TO LOOK LIKE A REAL
BOOK...

Minimal (art)/Modular (world)/Programmed (life)

Gerhard Richter

Lorna Simpson

Damien Hirst

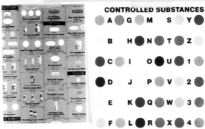

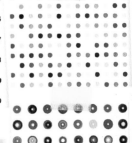

CONTROLLED SUBSTANCES

A	G	M	S	Y	5
B	H	N	T	Z	6
C	I	O	U	1	7
D	J	P	V	2	8
E	K	Q	W	3	9
F	L	R	X	4	0

Karel Martens

M–I X–Y

R–U B–Z

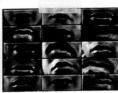

Donald Judd

Dan Flavin

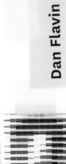

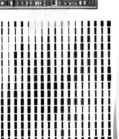

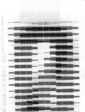

Form follow concept follow form

Tibor Kalman

John Baldessari

SOLVING EACH PROBLEM AS IT ARISES

IT CAN BE SUBJECT MATTER OF A RELIGIOUS NATURE, A SCENE IN A FOREIGN COUNTRY. WHATEVER THE SUBJECT, THE PROFESSIONAL ARTIST MAKES EXHAUSTIVE STUDIES OF IT. WHEN HE FEELS THAT HE HAS INTERPRETED THE SUBJECT TO THE EXTENT OF HIS CAPABILITIES HE MAY HAVE A ONE-MAN EXHIBITION WHOSE THEME IS THE SOLUTION OF THE PROBLEM. IT IS SURPRISING HOW FEW PEOPLE WHO VIEW THE PAINTINGS REALIZE THIS.

TIPS FOR ARTISTS WHO WANT TO SELL

• GENERALLY SPEAKING PAINTINGS WITH LIGHT COLORS SELL MORE QUICKLY THAN PAINTINGS WITH DARK COLORS.

• SUBJECTS THAT SELL WELL: MADONNA AND CHILD, LANDSCAPES, FLOWER PAINTINGS, STILL LIFES (FREE OF MORBID PROPS, DEAD BIRDS, ETC.), NUDES, MARINE PICTURES, ABSTRACTS AND SURREALISM.

• SUBJECT MATTER IS IMPORTANT: IT HAS BEEN SAID THAT PAINTINGS WITH COWS AND HENS IN THEM COLLECT DUST WHILE THE SAME PAINTINGS WITH BULLS AND ROOSTERS SELL.

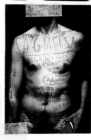

Stefan Sagmeister

Åbäke

my lord archbishop
your excellencies
your graces
my lords
ladies and
gentlemen
men and
women
children
embryos if any
spermatozoa reclining
at the
edge
of your
chairs

all living cells
bacteria
viruses
molecules of air and
dust and
water,

Jenny Holzer

ALL THINGS ARE
DELICATELY
INTERCONNECTED

SANDBERG
ANDBERG
NU NU
DBERG
BERG
ERG
RG
G

THE BEGINNING OF
THE WAR
WILL BE SECRET

I NEED TO LIE
BACK TO FRONT
WITH SOMEONE
WHO ADORES M

ORANGE

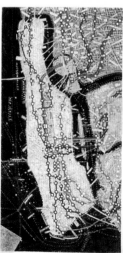

Paula Scher

Liam Gillick

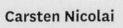

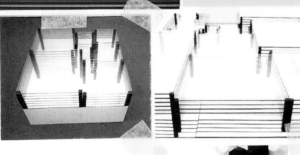

Massimo Vignelli

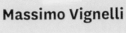

Carsten Nicolai

Ragnar Kjartansson

Antony Gormley

Alt group

A2/SW/HK

ONE DAY,
I WOULD LOVE
TO DESIGN...

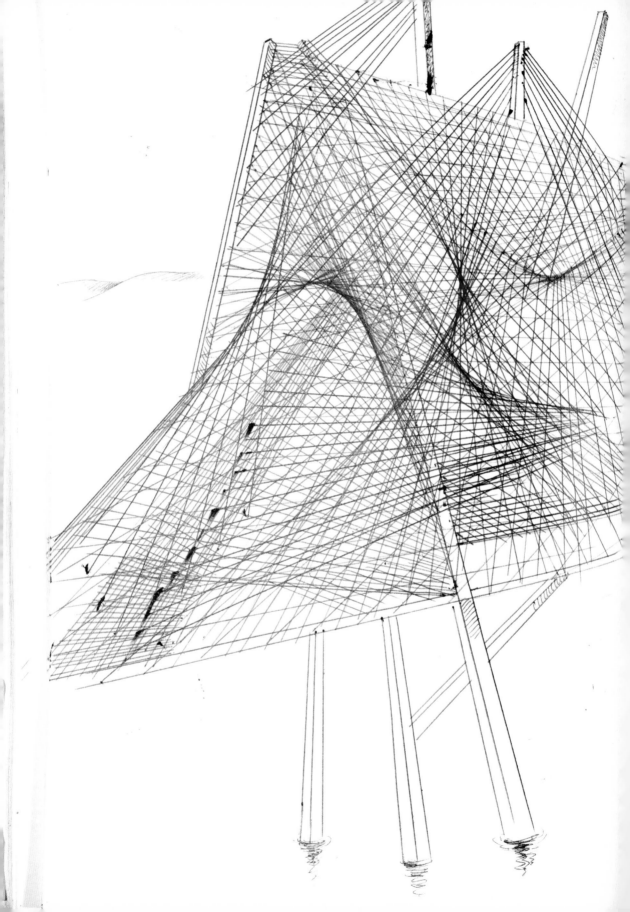

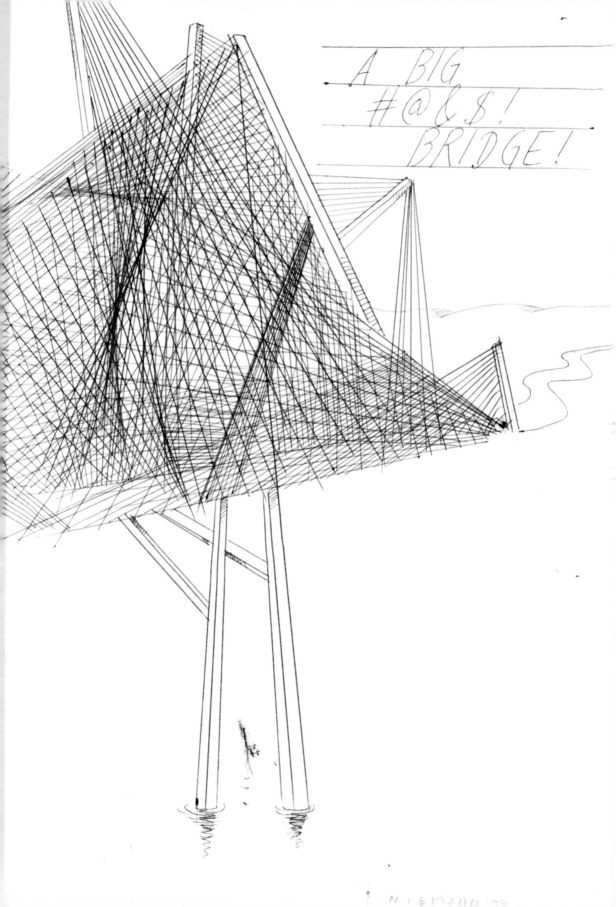

A BIG
#@&$!
BRIDGE!

NIEMANN '08

mk2010

in 2006 i conducted a six day event called
ROAM IS MY HOME. i occupied an exhibition space
in the CENTRAAL MUSEUM in Utrecht the netherlands
as my temporary New home. Ten projection screens

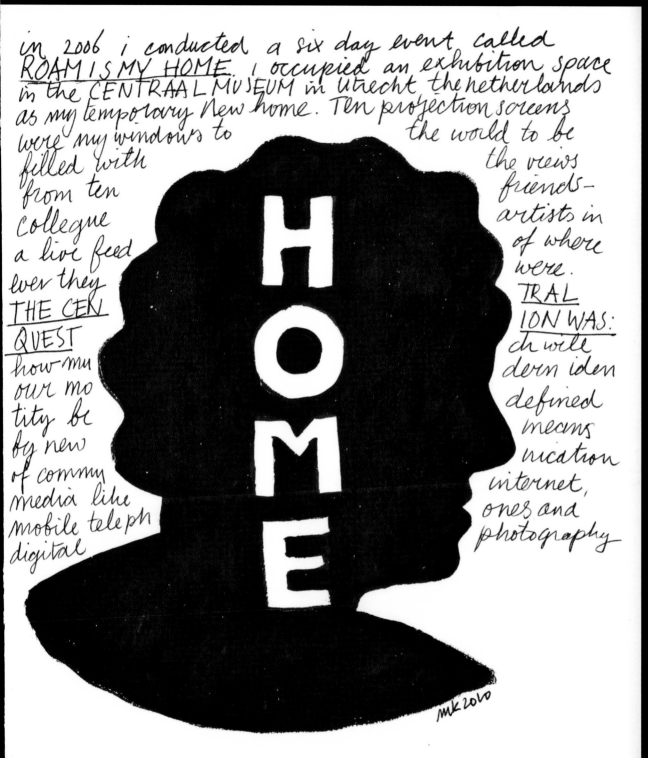

were my windows to   the world to be
filled with   the views
from ten   friends-
collegue   artists in
a live feed   of where
ever they   were.
THE CEN   TRAL
QUEST   ION WAS:
how-mu   ch will
our mo   dern iden
tity be   defined
by new   means
of commu   nication
media like   internet,
mobile teleph   ones and
digital   photography

mk 2010

A HOUSE IS LESS A HOME BUT A PLACE WHER COMMUNICATION
STREAMS MERGE THE HOUSE IS AN INFORMATION PORTAL MORE
THAN A PLACE OF SAFETY AND PRIVACY. MOBILE ELECTRONIC DEVICES
EXPAND OUR PERSONAL SPACE AND ENABLE US TO TAKE HOME
WITH US ANYWHERE AT ANYTIME.
ROAM IS MY HOME

① VIEW FROM ABOVE. WALL AT END USED FOR LIVE DRAWING/ART PROGRAMME

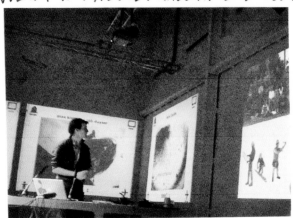 

② LIVE FEED FROM 10 REMOTE LOCATIONS ③ INTERACTING AUDIENCE

④ THE "ROAMING STORY WRITER" IS THE (CONJUNCTION) OF ROAM IS MY HOME AND STORYLINE™ ABOVE PICTURES ILLUSTRATE THE EXHIBITION SPACE OF ROAM IS MY HOME W/ TEN LIVE SCREEN PROJECTIONS A CENTRAL STAGE FOR PERFORMANCE AND PRESENTATION, INTERACTING AUDIENCE.

XAMPLES

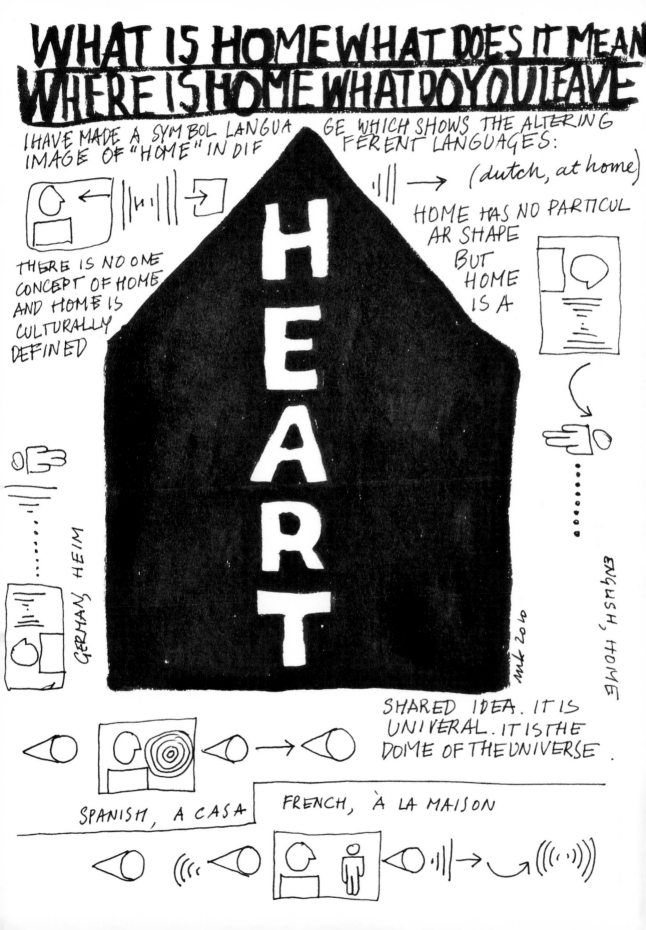

WHAT IS HOME WHAT DOES IT MEAN WHERE IS HOME WHAT DO YOU LEAVE

I HAVE MADE A SYMBOL LANGUAGE WHICH SHOWS THE ALTERING IMAGE OF "HOME" IN DIFFERENT LANGUAGES:

(dutch, at home)

HOME HAS NO PARTICULAR SHAPE BUT HOME IS A

THERE IS NO ONE CONCEPT OF HOME AND HOME IS CULTURALLY DEFINED

GERMAN, HEIM

ENGLISH, HOME

SHARED IDEA. IT IS UNIVERAL. IT IS THE DOME OF THE UNIVERSE.

SPANISH, A CASA

FRENCH, À LA MAISON

THE ROAM STORYWRITER

IS AN EDITORIAL ENVIRONMENT
AND NOT AN OPEN SOURCE ENVIRONMENT
MEANING ITS CONTENT AND CONTRIBUTERS ARE CURATED
AND MONITORED (ALTHOUGH THEY MONITOR THEMSELVES)

IT IS A MAGAZINE
OR AN EXHIBITION
IT IS AN EVENT

IT COULD BE A DAILY, OR A WEEKLY, BI-
WEEKLY, MONTHY. DEPENDING ON AVAILABLE
CONTRIBUTORS AND OTHER LOGISTICS. AND
MAYBE THE UNLIMITED BUDGET.

FOR 10 ~~IMAGE~~ VISUAL (& SOUND) BLOGS (STREAMS,
THREADS, I WOULD HIRE (52 X 10 = 520) ARTISTS,
VISUAL CONTRIBUTORS, AUTHORS AND SUCH; EVERY
WEEK A NEW DIFFERENT TEAM. ~~FOR THE TWO~~
THESE CONTRIBUTORS PREFERABLE DON'T RESIDE ON
THE LOCATION THEY USUALLY CALL HOME.
THEY ARE ROAMING

FOR THE TWO TEXT CHANNELS I WOULD INVITE
AS MUCH AS POSSIBLE CONTRIBUTORS TO PROVIDE
A CONTINOUS FLOW OF POETRY AND METAPHORES
THE OPERATE FROM THE STABLE LOCATION OF THE
INSTALLATION/EXHIBITION SPACE. WHETHER THE ARE
LOCAL OR VISITORS.

ALL WORK AND CONTRIBUTIONS WILL
BE ARCHIVED AND TRANSFORMED INTO
A MOVIE, BROADCAST OR OTHER
DYNAMIC PRESENTATION

IN CONTRAST TO INDIVIDUAL EXPERIENCE ON AN
INDIVIDUAL DEVICE. THIS IS A SHARED
EXPERIENCE ONLY. LIKE OLD FASHION ED TV

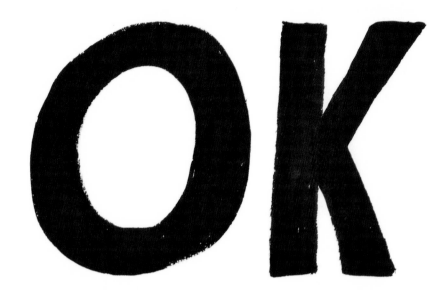

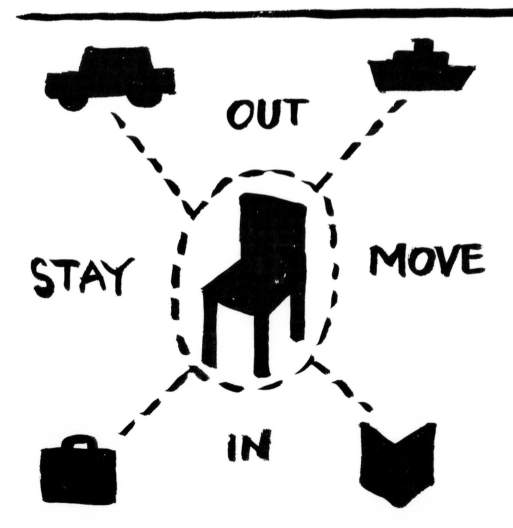

STORYLINE IS BASICALLY A LIMITED
TYPEWRITER FOR SHORT POETRY
(AS FAR AS I AM CONCERNED) · LOOK FOR YOUR OWN
METAPHORES TO EXPRES
DUALITY

IT WORKS LIKE THIS (SORT OF)

POET 1 ON LOCATION 1

① TYPE YOUR POEM

⑬ RESPOND TO RESPOND POEM

③ BROADCAST YOUR POEM

② READ YOUR POEM

HELLO THERE THIS

④ READ YOUR POEM

⑫ RESPOND POEM DISPLAYED

⑪ RESPOND POEM TRANSLATED

TRANS LATE

⑤ YOUR POEM TRANSLATED

⑦ YOUR POEM BEING READ

⑧ RESPOND TO POEM IN OTHER LANGUAGE

POET 2 ON LOCATION

THE LIMITATION OF TEXT LENGTH ENFORCES CLARITY

⑥ YOUR POEM TRANSLATED DISPLAYED

⑩ RESPOND POEM BEING DISPLAYED

⑨ BROADCAST RESPOND POEM

mvk 2010

THE PURPOSE OF THE STORY LINE SCREEN IS TO GET A GRAPHIC (B&W!) APPEALING VISUAL TEXTURE (RATHER THAN BORING TYPE)

ACTUALLY EACH SCREEN HAS ITS OWN CPU (COMPUTER). EACH LOCATION HAS ONE CENTRAL SERVER THAT CONTROLS THESE CPU'S (SLAVES). THE TEXTS (ONE GLYPH ON ONE SCREEN) ARE DISTRIBUTED BY HTTP PROTOCOL OVER A LOCAL IP NETWORK. THE TEXT ALSO IS SEND OVER THE INTERNET TO A REMOTE LOCATION PASSING THE TRANSLATION MACHINE

BECAUSE ITS MODULAR SET UP THE SYSTEM IS FLEXIBLE AND EXPANDABLE. IT ALSO OFFERS A VARIETY OF OUTPUT OPTIONS: SMALLER OR LARGER SCREENS, OR EVEN PROJECTION

EACH SCREEN IS OPERATED BY ITS OWN CPU/COMPUTER AS SLAVES OF A CENTRAL COMPUTER/SERVER THAT DISTRIBUTES THE GLYPHS TO THE INDIVIDUAL SCREENS/CPU'S

THIS LINE IS A STORY TOO

VERY SIMPLE GRID FOR GLYPH COVERING AS MUCH AS POSSIBLE SCREEN SPACE ESTATE

THE ASPECT RATIO OF THE SCREENS USE IS THE ONLY RESTRICTION FOR THE GLYPH/FONT DESIGN.

ROAM IS MY HOME WOULD RUN FROM A SERVER TO ENABLE
10 ARTIST TO FEED THEIR OWN CHANNELS, VISITORS TO
RESPOND AND INTERACT, GENERATE DYNAMIC OUTPUT
FOR EACH CHANNEL /ARTIST IN THE EXHIBITION TO BE
PROJECTED AND MAINTAIN AND UPDATE THE WEBSITE
WITH CURRENT CHANGES AND INFORMATION.

DATABASE

1 2 3 4 5 6 7 8 9 10

ARTIST'S
DYNAMIC OUTPUT
CHANNEL
IN EXHIB
SPACE

ARTIST
INPUT/OUTPUT

VISITOR INPUT/
OUTPUT

SERVER
OPENSOURCE FORUM
SOFTWARE HTML
MYSQL

ADMIN

WWW
GENERAL INFO
ARTISTS +
OUTPUT

A SITE FOR ARTISTS AND TO CREATE
A FORUM "THREAD" WITH IMAGES, TEXTS AND SOUNDS
VISITORS ARE ABLE RESPOND WITH IMAGES, TEXTS AND SOUNDS.

I LIGHT A FIRE AND THE FLAMES ARE BRIGHT
THE STARS ARE HIGH IN THE SKY TONIGHT
A DISTANT TRAIN BLOWS A DISTANT HORN
AND I AM FAR AWAY FROM HOME

MY BAG IS EMPTY AND I AM BROKE
I'M LOOKING FOR SHELTER BUT THE DOORS
ARE CLOSE

I HEAR YOU SAY BABY PLEASE DON'T GO
BUT I AM FAR AWAY FROM HOME

WHERE I AM ROAMING
THERE I WILL BE
WHERE I AM GOING
THERE I WILL SLEEP
WHERE I AM SITTING
THERE I WILL EAT
BUT ALL I REALLY
WANT TO DO
IS BE WITH YOU

I DRIVE MY CAR THROUGH THE LONELY NIGHT
I LOOK AROUND AND I WONDER WHY
THE DAY APPEARS IN A PALE BLUE DOME
AND I AM FAR AWAY FROM HOME

(DEC. 2008) MK 2008

IS WHERE THE IS

MK 2010

IF I HAD AN UNLIMITED BUDGET I'D PICK UP THE
PROJECT AND WOULD DEVELOP IT TO IT'S NEXT LEVEL

THE FOCUS IS TO CREATE AN ENVIRONMENT
OF CONTEMPLATION. CONNECTIVITY WOULD BE THE
KEY AND SERINITY ITS SOUL.

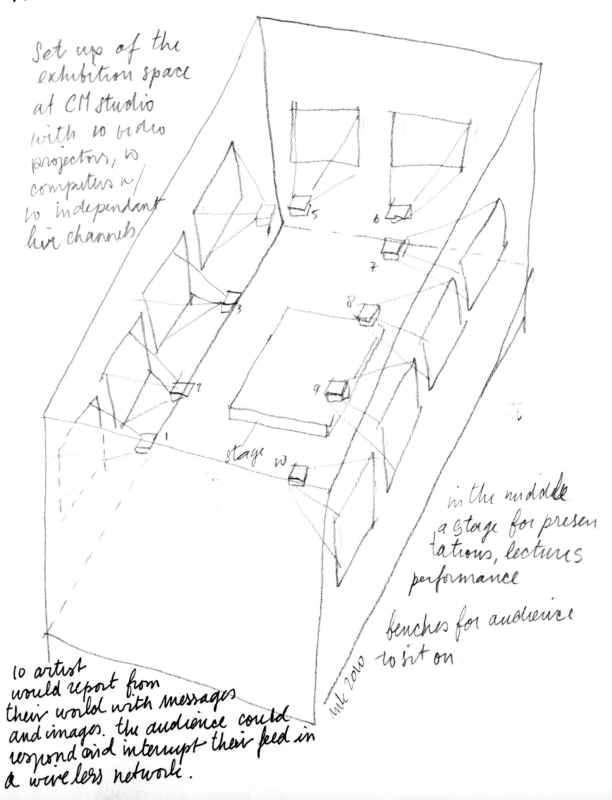

Set up of the
exhibition space
at CM studio
with 10 video
projectors, 10
computers w/
10 independant
live channels

in the middle
a stage for presen
tations, lectures
performance

benches for audience
to sit on

stage

10 artist
would report from
their world with messages
and images. the audience could
respond and interrupt their feed in
a wireless network.

SAMPLES OF STUDIES AND EXPERI
MENTS INVOLVING THE STORYLINE
PROJECT. ① POSTER DESIGNS
"ART MUST MOVE" IN ENGLISH AND ARABIC FOR NEW YORK BASED
PERFORMA 2009 FESTIVAL ② PICTURE FRAMES: 4 LETTER WORDS (UNSYN
CHRONIZED) ③ PICTURE FRAMES VARIOUS FORMATS ④ ARCHITECTURAL
DESIGN FOR STORYLINE ENVIRONMENT (HISHAM YOUSSEE) ⑤ ARABIC
VERSION OF STORYLINE FONT (NAJI EL MIR) ⑥ MIX OF CAPS AND LOW
CASE IN LATIN VERSION (MAX KISMAN) ⑦ WORKING PROTOTYPE (BULKY)
BY WIEL SEVSKENS (NIMK, AMSTERDAM)

I WOULD BUY ALL BOOKS AND FREE THE CAPTURED BIRDS

STOŁECZNA
2,50 zł

gazeta
WYBORCZA.PL

CO KRYJĄ LOCHY LECHA

Wiemy, co urzędnicy prezydenta Lecha Kaczyńskiego chowają w czeluściach jego kancelarii. To nagrania zeznań oficerów WSI, polityków i innych osób składane przed komisją weryfikacyjną Macierewicza

Najdłuższy i najwyższy most w Polsce

Punctuality is the thief of time

Not / to decide is to decide.

We are tomorrow's PAST.

He lived his life to the end.

LUST

I am writting this letter slowly, as I know you do not read quickly.

I am writting to tell you I have nothing to say.

Visual intimacy

Of mood

12

The moment of recognising your own lack of talent is a flash of genius.

I am not sincere, not even when I say I am not.

Often it is fatal to live too long.

↓ DOWN

WITH GRAVITY

ALL THIS RELAXATION HAS EXHAUSTED ME.

I've got a good memory for forgetting

QUICK AS A FLASHLIGHT

That is as clear as mud.

THINK FORE YOU HINK!

OF DOOD

The UNNATURAL, THATS TOO is NATURAL

lust

LUST

I had a monumental idea this morning, but I didn't like it.

IMONI EXTRA

A LOE DOODLES

LUST

I wish he would explain his explanation.

The exit is usually where the entrance was.

Vladimir CHAIKA

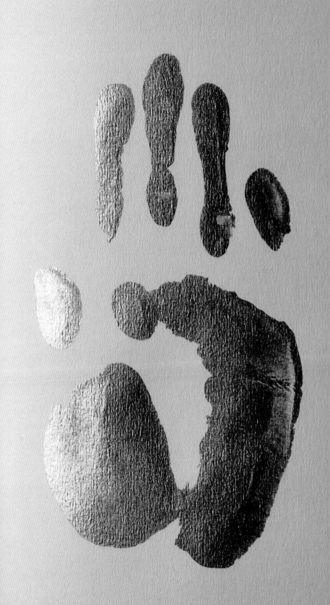

TEXT FROM:
TRUMAN CAPOTE
FIRST AND LAST / MASTER MISERY
PENGUEN 60's, 1995

HELVETICA COND. 9 PT.
MAJ. MIN.

HOMAGE TO MAESIN

GARAMOND ITALIC 12 pt.
MAJ. MIN.

As he opened the door, Miss Mozart appeared, her starched uniform rustling drily in the hall. 'We hope you will return,' she said, and handed Sylvia a sealed envelope. **'Mr Revercomb was most particularly pleased.'**

2

'I don't know how to tell about it. It's so odd. But – well, I had lunch at the Automat today, and I had to share the table with these three men. I might as well have been invisible because they talked about the most personal things. One of the men said his girl friend was going to have a baby and he didn't know where he was going to get the money to do anything about it. So one of the other men asked him why didn't he sell something. He said he didn't have anything to sell. Whereupon the third man (he was rather delicate and didn't look as if he belonged with the others) said yes, there was something he could sell: dreams.

'That was sensible of you,' said Estelle as she began stacking dishes in the kitchen sink. 'Imagine what might have happened. Buying dreams! Whoever heard! Uh uh, honey, this sure isn't Easton.'

The envelope Miss Mozart had handed her: it was in the purse, and until now she had forgotten it. She tore it open. Inside there was a blue note folded around a bill; on the note there was written:

In payment of one dream, $5.

3

And now she believed it; it was true, and she had **sold Mr Revercomb a dream.** Could it be really so simple as that? She laughed a little as she turned off the light again. If she were to sell a dream only twice a week, think of what she could do: a place some-where all her own, she thought, deepening towards sleep, ease, like firelight, wavered over her, and there came the moment of twilit lantern slides, deeply deeper.

The sonofabitch, he is a thief and a threat: he will take everything you have and end by leaving you

'I've been other things besides a clown. I have sold insurance, too.'

'Oh?' said Sylvia, disappointed. 'And what do you do now?'

Oreilly chuckled and threw his ball especially high; after the catch his head still remained tilted upward. 'I watch the sky,' he said. 'There I am with my suitcase travelling through the blue. It's where you travel when you've got no place else to go. But what do I do on this planet? I have stolen, begged, and **sold my dreams** – all for purposes of whiskey.

nothing, not even a dream.

Today she would tell Mr Revercomb about the three blind children. He would like that. The prices he paid varied, and she was sure this was at least a **ten-dollar dream.**

Yossi LEMEL

26

Be

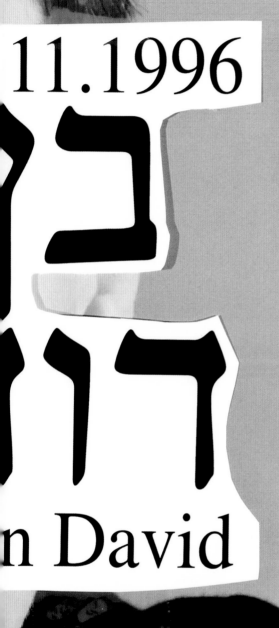

11.1996

בן דוד

n David

I would like to make a journey of discovery to document the story of my family. It is a project of photography and text creating a historic and epic convergence. On one side my mother and my father - both Holocaust survivors - and their family, Polish Jews who were dispersed around the world after World War II. They went to live in the US, France, Belgium and Israel. Part of them are ultra-orthodoxe Jews, others fighting for secular freedom. On the other side is the story of my wife's family, a German family with ties to the Nazi war machine. Her family was scattered around the world as well after World War II, to the US, Brazil and some European countries. The fruitful meeting between the two families, which created our four children, carries the message of a bridge to the future between nations and people.
Yossi Lemel
Tel Aviv Israel 2010.

Yossi Lemel

Noa Tamara

22.6.2000

הצייה
נת

Daniel Nathan

14.7.2007

יונתן
ישי

Jonathan Yishai

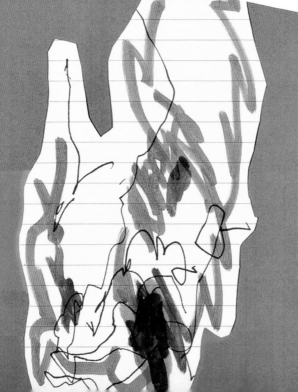

the
inspiration
from

by Wang Xu

shape, materials, size, color and time can bring up everlasting product. regarding *LUST* project, my thinking is started from "minimum" concept. i use the way of subtraction to do testing on some products which are mature or well-known by consumers. by deleting the visual information one by one on the product - such as logo, types and texts, only keep the original shape and color of the product remained, just like fruit. in such way, the product can be identified? the product information could be transferred? anyway, it is what i want to attempt and it is the lust i want to redesign to some products.

5 67

1 0

2 1 0 4

4 3 4 3   ㅇ ㅏ ㄴ ㅅ ㅏ ㅇ ㅅ ㅜ   A H N

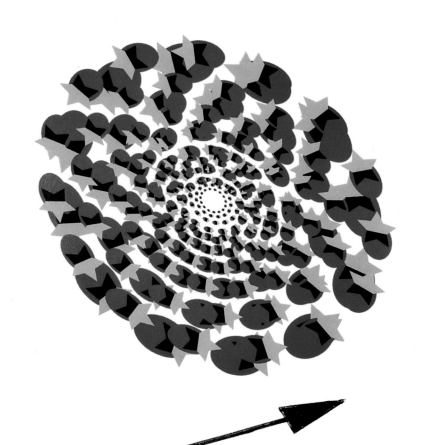

Keep watching!

Keizo Matsui

It takes 1,000 years to remove all the land mines from the earth.

Keizo Matsui

Things to do when I make my millions from Australian graphic design magazine. Land a cust[omer]... my students. Design vinyl album sleeves. Comic Sans the movie - make it a reality. Int[o] definitive history of Australian Graphic Design. Make us reflex blue again. Compensate Neville Brody. slavish imitation of their work, when I was a s[tudent]... Just sit around a draw pictures all day like n[ormal]... from Graphic Designer to 'Information Architect'. Buy... Have exotic foreign interns work for me. Make the... starring Daniel Day Lewis called 'There Will Be [Blood?]... for local bands. Don't take no shit from the 'n[ame?]... 'bigger'. Afford to enter some design awards and... pieces aren't accepted. Sell a logo to a client that... anything that Brian Eno wants me to. Create... use an illustrator or photographer on some jobs. else to design me a business card. Take a yea[r]... my monograph the 'heaviest'. Learn not to tak[e]... first graphic designer in space (outer, not int[erior]... Real World Records and change their album c[over]... front' style. Have Steve Heller write about m[e]...

graphic design: Create an inspirational
teaching job and bask in the adoration of
tart a brewery (design the labels, win, win!)
for a studio in New York. Compile the
we for certain that less is more. Never have to
avid Carson and Charles S Anderson for my
dent. **Offer** to design peoples lost pet notices.
parents think I do now. Change my job title
my way into the Type Directors' Annual.
efinitive film of my struggles as a graphic Designer
s 032'. **Design** AO sized screenprinted posters
n. **Never** ever have to make a clients logo
t care about losing the money when the
basically just a black square. **Design**
y own line of Adidas sneakers. Afford to
ange my name to 'Christoff'. Get someone
f from designing on the computer. **Make**
it so personally (or seriously). **Be the**
'). Direct a video for Bjork. **Buy**
er design back to the 'no type' on the
Work on some vanity projects. Remember to be humble

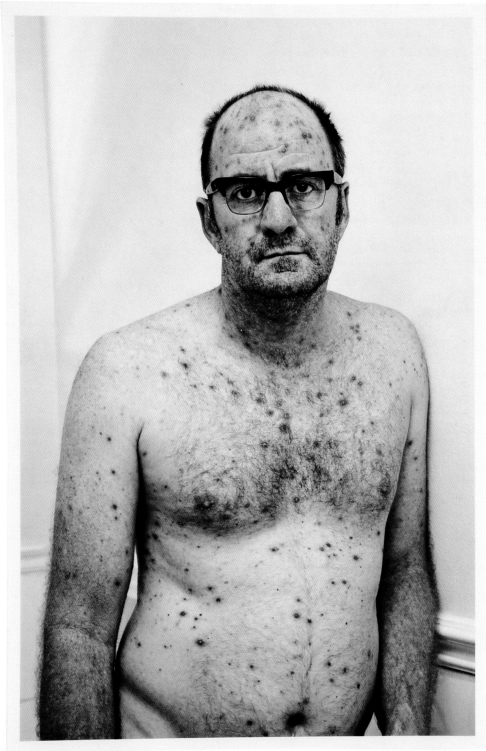

SELF PORTRAIT WITH CHICKENPOX   GARTH WALKER ©

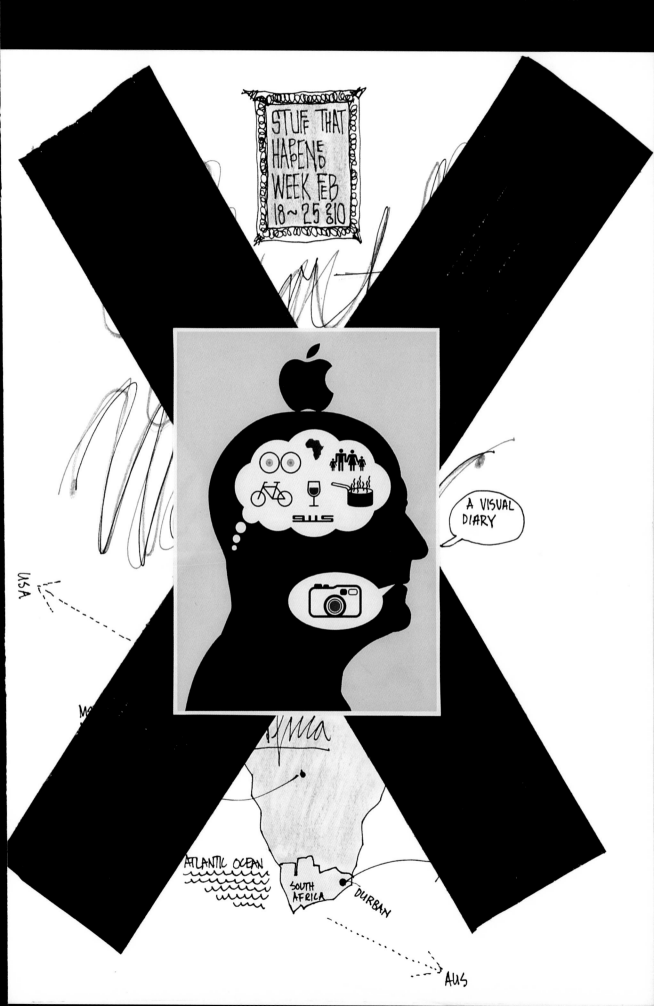

BRUSH + INK
DRAWING
SUNDAY FEB 21

I became obsessed with photography at art school in the 70's. This old Leica hangs on my bedroom door next to my bed. I find it looking over me very comforting — like an old frien I have something like seven different camera systems, bu this old Leica is my favourite. The stories it could tell...

Years ago, I read an article in which the world's super über photographers were asked to name the '10 iconic cameras of all time'. The list included the Linhof Technika, Hasselblad, Nikon F, Leica M3 and so on. But the odd one out was the Olympus Trip 35. Reason being it has a century old Zeiss designed 40mm razor sharp lens, and all mechanical light meter and idiot proof handling. Olympus made 12 million of them over 20 years. I found mine in Cape Town late last year, in mint condition with its pouch and lens cap for $25. A test roll revealed serious light leaks, so a bit of velvet ribbon and some contact glue and "she is fixed". I carry it around when I'm out of town, and shoot whatever happens to be in front of the camera at the time. This is the next roll I've just had processed. Fuck me, I love this thing!

I was recently invited to exhibit at a Biennale in France — these were some of the posters relating to the exhibition theme. around concerns facing Africans into the future, plus some satirical comments on the history of French armament industry...

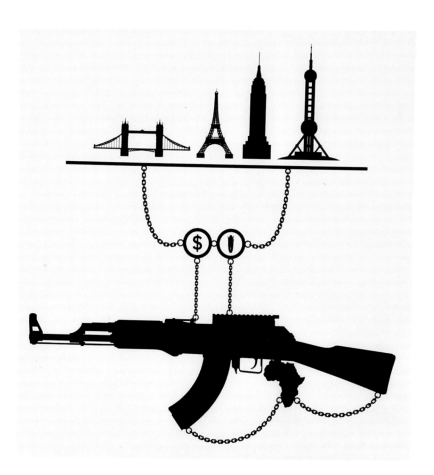

UN EXOCET

UN EXOCET

Particupation is the new currency of loyalty

LAVATORIES ARE FITTED WITH SMOKE DETECTORS

Couple next to me. Late 30's. She bit 'dried out' but nice tits. He looks 'Hooray Henry' type. Don't exchange a single word all meal. Are they fighting? Dissillusioned? They get up to leave. He pays. She then gives him half in cash. He takes the money and trousers it. I then notice the wedding rings. Are they married?

Quick coffee at Vida. Guy walks in, sits down. Girlfriend (?) arrives. Sits down. Quick smooch. She gets up to go to the loo. He sits there looking forlorn. Suddenly, out of the blue, his nose starts to bleed. Very red against his skin. He picks up a napkin and holds up to nose. Gets up and walks out, passing girlfriend en route. Waives to her and continues walking.

We are not in the design business. We are in the opinion business...

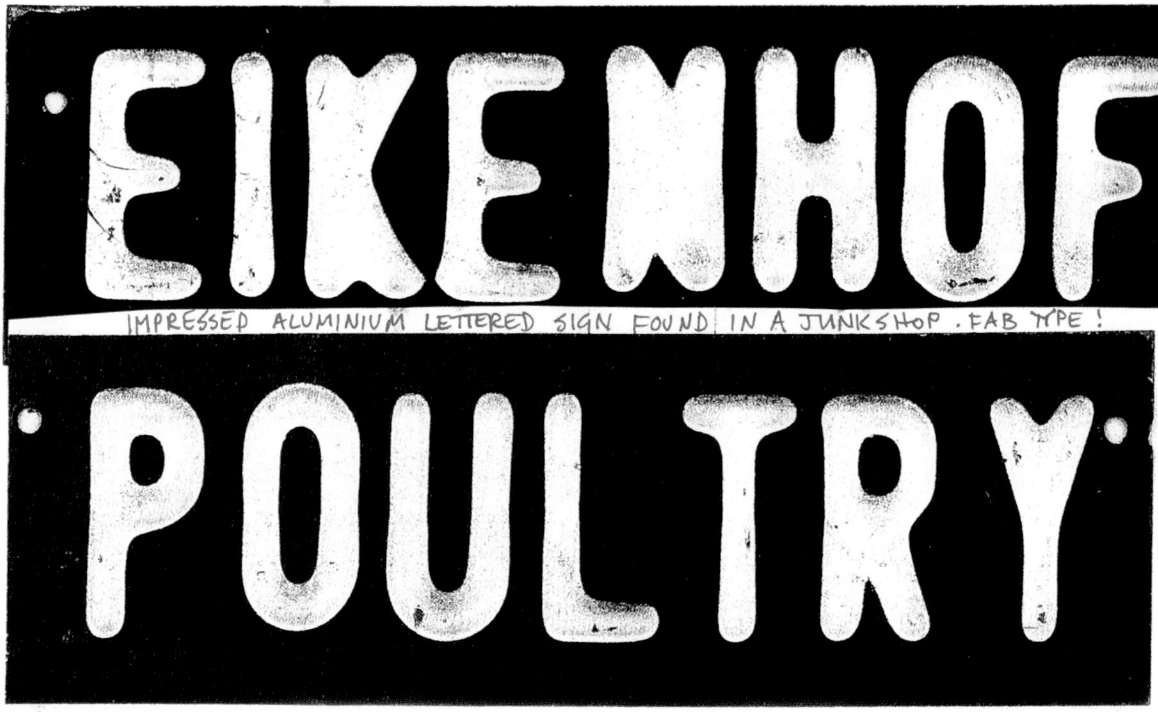

EIKENHOF

IMPRESSED ALUMINIUM LETTERED SIGN FOUND IN A JUNKSHOP. FAB TYPE!

POULTRY

Charles H "Chuck" Taylor who played the Akron Firestones walked into Converse complaining of sore feet.

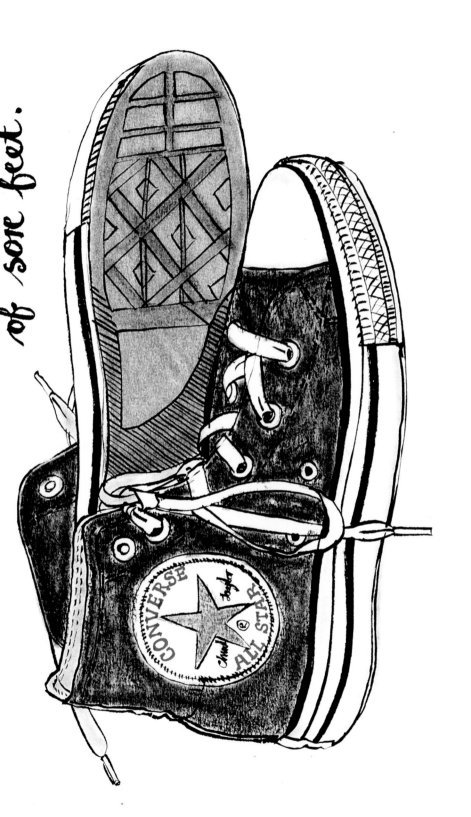

CONVERSE ALL STAR

Chuck Taylor

158

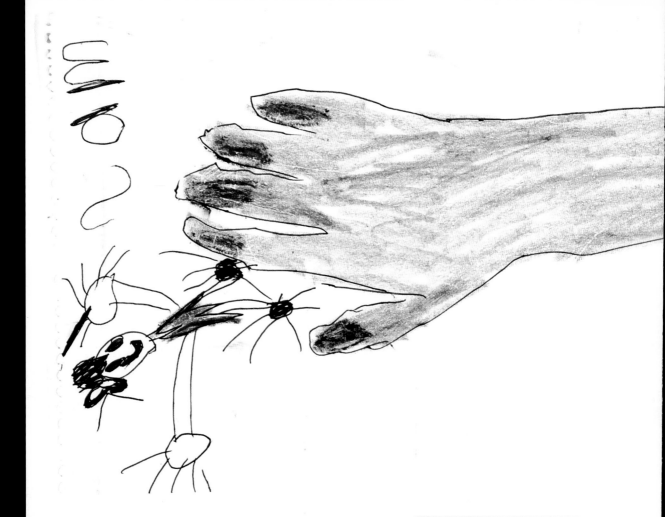

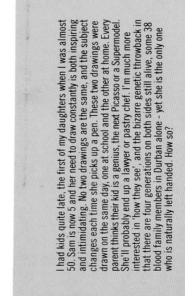

I had kids quite late, the first of my daughters when I was almost 50. Sam is now 5 and her need to draw constantly is both inspiring and intimidating. No two drawings are the same, and the subject changes each time she picks up a pen. These two drawings were drawn on the same day, one at school and the other at home. Every parent thinks their kid is a genius, the next Picasso or a Supermodel. She'll probably end up a lawyer or pastry chef. I'm much more interested in 'how they see', and the bizarre genetic throwback in that there are four generations on both sides still alive, some 38 blood family members in Durban alone - yet she is the only one who is naturally left handed. How so?

Typical African Patent medicine Packaging. Insane, isnt it!

RHEUMATIC MIXTURE

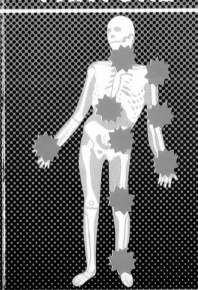

UMUTHI WAMALUNGU ABUHLUNGU

Contains TARTRAZINE

PLEASE READ ENCLOSED PACKAGE INSERT CAREFULLY.

SHAKE THE BOTTLE BEFORE USE

200 ml

RHEUMATIC MIXTURE
Reference No.
C702 (Act 101/1965)

COMPOSITION:
Each 15 ml contains:
Aqueous extracts of:
Apium graveolens........14,10 mg
Achillea millefolium......30,50 mg
Arctostaphylos
  uva ursi..................46,80 mg
Trifolium pratense.......30,50 mg
Rhamnus purshiana ...21,00 mg
Populus tremoides .....30,50 mg
Agrimonia eupatoria ...30,50 mg
Anacyclus pyrethrum ..30,50 mg
Preserved with:
Methyl paraben..........0.2%m/v
Propyl paraben..........0.05%m/v

ADULTS DOSAGE:
Three medicine
measuresful (15 ml) to be
taken with water, three
times a day after meals.

**STORAGE
INSTRUCTIONS:**
Store in a cool place below
25 °C. Avoid exposure to
direct sunlight.

KEEP OUT OF REACH OF
CHILDREN.

Applicant/Applikant
African Medicines (Pty) Ltd
68 Rigger Road/weg 68
Spartan
Kempton Park, 1618

UF01-020
03/2004
Britepak

RHEUMATIC MIXTURE

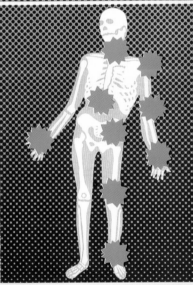

MORIANA WA MANONYELETSO A BOHLOKO

R20·00

6 002852 001406

Bauhaus is King. This is the wood rimmed steering wheel of my 1968 Porsche 911S, one of only two imported into South Africa that year. It's totally original and never been restored, save for a repaint long before my time. Nothing on the planet drives like this car, and I've driven a few. I also have a 1989 911 Carrera - obscene I know...

SOME THINGS I LIKE...

+ the fur magnet

I've been a lifelong cyclist, both MTB and road. As an impoverished graphic designer (nothing's changed) in the late 70s and early 80s, this Vitus first generation aluminium-frame with Campy groupset was state of the art, and ridden by teams in the Tour De France. I've been buying bikes like this for a while and now have six. I ride them all at least 5 times a week and MTB on weekends

Freedom
Is Illegal

Stickering
Is Something
You Take

Let's
our

marry*

deas

*you can always get divorced and run away with a new one!

Los padres de Cocteau

Minta Bus nelli
Noemí Frenkel
maría Alché

ADAPTACIÓN: IGNACIO APOLO
ESCENOGRAFÍA: JORGE FERRARI
VESTUARIO: ANDREA MERCADO / ILUMINACIÓN: ELI SIRLING
PRODUCCIÓN EJECUTIVA: MP PRODUCCIONES

**ESTRENO 19 DE ABRIL 21:00 HS
TEATRO EL CUBO
ZELAYA 3056, ABASTO**

FUNCIONES JUEVES, VIERNES Y SÁBADOS 21:00 HS
DOMINGOS 19:00 HS / INFORMES: 49632568

EL CUBO
teatro · performance · danza

TICKETEK.COM
Tel: 5237 7200

AMO MI LIVING

«Les Parents Terribles» Theatre play by Jean Cocteau.
Still love this rejected poster.

terribles
Luis Machín
Nahuel Pérez Biscayart
dirección:
Alejandra Ciurlanti
EL FANTASMA DE HEREDIA / 07
MITRE
AM 790
TCC
bizarro
NÓMADE

Rico LINS

O HOMEM QUE VIROU BODE

AUTOR DILA

CASA NATIVA

PIPOCA

JFK

P A

JFK
NEW YORK (KENNE

PAN A

SOUVENIR OF VISIT TO THE MOST FAMOUS BUILDING IN THE WORLD

EMPIRE STATE
OBSERVATORIES

TERROR
IS
ME

ADULT INTELLECTUALS ONLY! FOR

Cole
Porter
USA
29

By air mail
Par avion

39
40

025566
INDIANA TICKET
025566

A ORIGINAL

FAX (681) 2-00

CERILLOS LA PAZ, S. A. de C.V.

CAÑON DEL COBRE,
CH. HUAHUA.

LINS/RICARDO

LIHUE

KAHULUI

ALOHA AIRLINES INC

AQ 228 N11MAR 630P

**** 610P OPEN

THANK YOU FOR FLYING
ALOHA AIRLINES
J17

Quejas
Complains

Revise su equi
Check your ba
Ne oubliez pas
bagages

Tarifa Autoriz
(Ud. no tiene que

Authorized Fa
(You don't have

Tarif Autorise
(ne payez plus)

Talón usuario

RESERVACIONES EN:
P. O. BOX 159
LOS MOCHIS, SIN., MEXICO

B
Balderrama
HOTELES
Y TOURS

CIERRESE ANTES DE ENCENDER.

Transportación
Terrestre

Zona
Zone
2

ZON
5
$ 16,000
Derecho uso de P
I. V. A. Incluido
$ 2,100
R.F.C. ASA-680010

Nº 258607 A

ر محمد الخامس / الدار البيضاء

AEROPORT MOHAMMED V / CASABLAN

№ 4100880 · تذكرة سفر رقم
Bulletin de Voyage

التاريخ السّاعة
Date _____ Heure _____

20 DH درهم

Timbre payé sur état
décision n°90 du 1-3-83

FILM Stockholm FESTIVAL

UDZIAŁ
W PRZEGLĄDZIE
OBOWIĄZKIEM
KAŻDEJ SŁUŻBY WS

III

PRZEGLĄD FILMÓW
AMATORSKICH ZUS HIEMIA

OŚWIĘCIM 19

Havana Club

23

星期五 FRIDAY 廿三

忌 宜

THE FINEST JAPAN GEKKEIKA
ENJOYING THE
SERVING BY THE IMP
PRODUCED AND
GEKKEIKAN SAK
FUSHIMI, KY

PANORAMA

blur

日本独占発売
2枚組特別価格

TOCP-50444-5
KROCK/POP STEREO
2枚組
定価3,262円（本体3,107）

STANDBY

GRAFICA 360°

**SI VES ALGO,
DI ALGO**
ctividad o paquete sospe
forma o tren, no te qued

**LIBERTAD
PRESXS**

TMB
Ferrocarril Metropolità de Barcelona, S.A.

N.º C.I.F. A08 005 795
BILLET SENZILL
Tarifa vigent, inclosa IVA IAOV
Per presentar a petició de qualsevol
empleat. Conserveu-lo fins a la sortida. **Sèrie 6B**
287914

WORD WALL WEB

HELL BANK NOTE

5000

№I 912345

VER DESTE LADO

Yen Soon

Yu Wong

DOLLARS

CHEE SHING PAPER MERCHANTS

IF I HAD
All the $$
IN the world...

I'd Buy this
Building ➤

(which is, strangely,
privately, owned.)

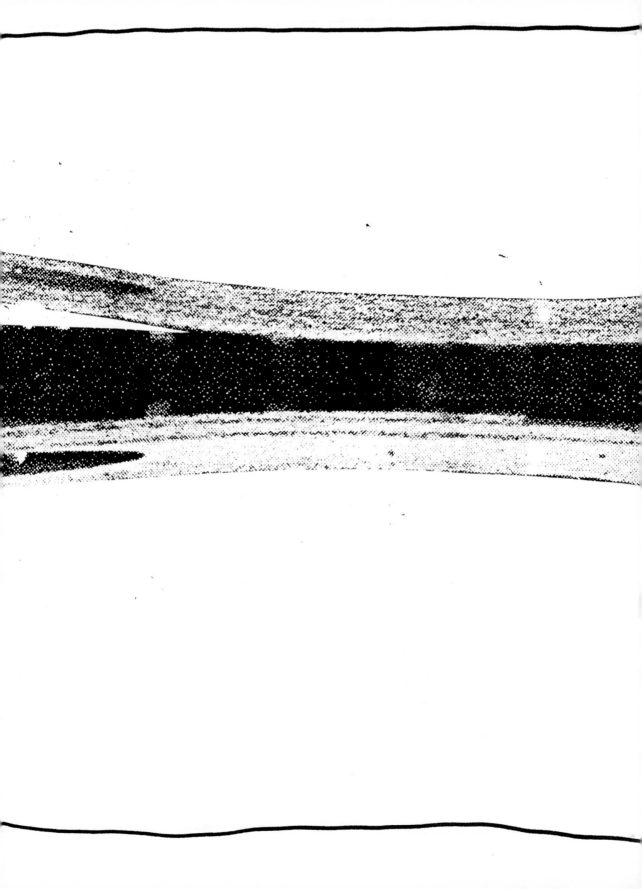

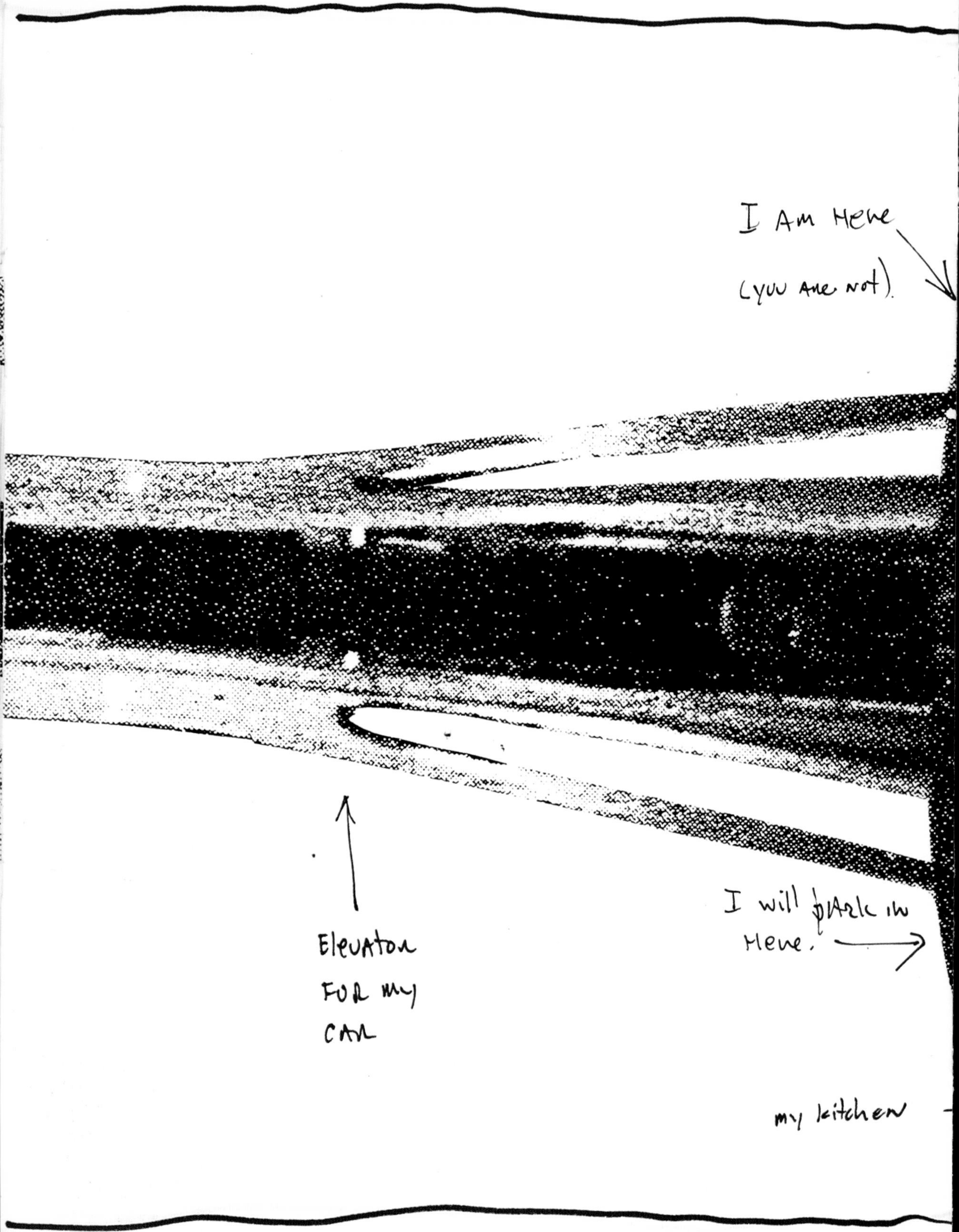
I AM HERE
(YOU ARE NOT)
I will PARK in HERE.
ELEVATOR FOR MY CAR
my kitchen

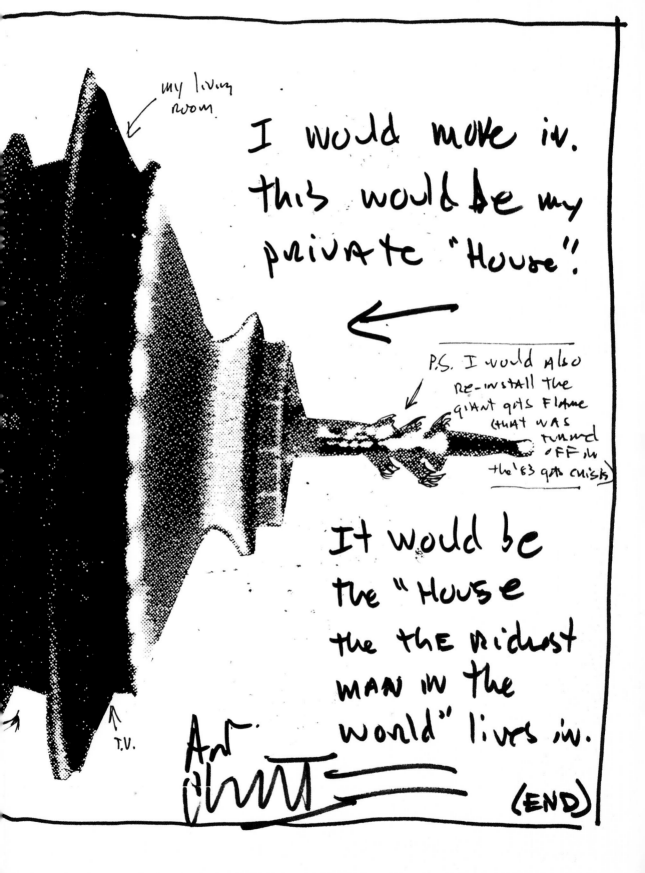

Rick VALICENTI

IN THIS WORLD OF OURS EVERY MESSAGE
HAS BEEN DESIGNED AND/OR BROADCAST
AT LEAST ONCE.

I IMAGINE DEVOTING
THE REST
OF MY LIFE
TO DESIGNING
OPPORTUNITIES
FOR A
UTOPIA
OF DO-GOODERS WHERE
EVERYTHING MADE
RETURNS ONE
HEARTFELT
RESPONSE

THE NEEDS
OF PEOPLE EVERYWHERE
WILL BE SATISFIED
AND DELIGHTED BY
UTOPIAN DO-GOODERS'
GOODS &
SERVICES

GENEROSITY AND UN-SELFISH BEHAVIOR WILL FLOURISH AND BECOME THE FOREVER-FORM OF CURRENCY.

NO CADRE OF GREEDY CROOKED BANKERS COULD EVER BRING DOWN THIS NEW ECONOMY.

THE LUST
FOR BRANDED
COMPETITION
VANISHES
INTO THIN
AIR OF
SMOKE AND
MIRRORS
IT CAME.

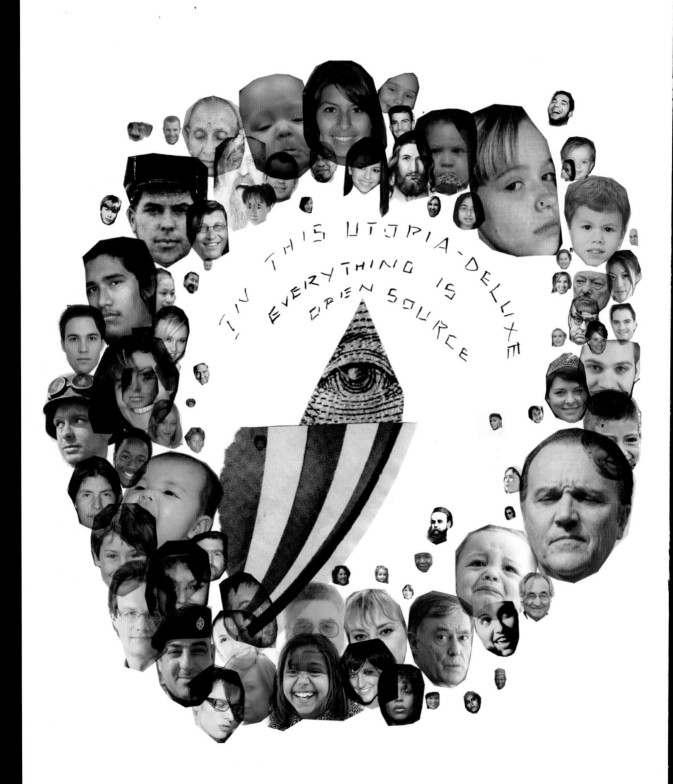

IN THIS UTOPIA-DELUXE EVERYTHING IS OPEN SOURCE

James VICTORE / Brooklyn, New York, **8**

What were your inspirations for this project?

I have always wanted to find a patron, someone willing to put up the dough to print and hang posters and billboards with purely social and cultural messages. I have always felt that design is a tool for powerful and positive change and I just need to find the right kind of crazy person with money to help me create sexy, memorable work for real people.

Does your passion get you in trouble?

I wish I actually got in trouble, real trouble with my work ... such as getting arrested for it. Then I would know I was doing something right.

Are there enough people following their lust?

If you look around stores and magazines and watch TV, it does not feel as though many people are having much fun.

Do you love what you do?

Immensely. And I also try not to take it seriously.

Why is it important to have an opinion and put it in the work?

Graphic design without an opinion is like people without opinions—bland and boring. Also, having the option of inserting my opinion in the work engages me fully with the project, making it more interesting to both me and the audience.

Mike PERRY / Brooklyn, New York, **12**

What makes you get out of bed?

Life. Making things!

There seems to be an ecological or organic feel to your work. Can you elaborate on this?

I like to just let things happen, and that has a tendency to create an organic feel. In addition, I love nature.

Are you doing what you love?

Big-time.

Would pursuing this lust as a job make you happy?

Currently doing it!

Are you a dreamer?

At night, no. During the day, all the time.

You have a strong reputation for making things by hand. Do you feel that, in these cookie-cutter, computer-driven, clip art-heavy times, that handmade is somehow new or cuts through the clutter?

Handmade is never new and always new. It has been happening forever and will always continue as long as we have hands. So, I have a hard time saying that it is new and really just look at it as what I need to do. I also remember that it is not always the answer. Sometimes, using the computer is the right answer. And remember, in the wrong hands hand-drawn can easily go cookie-cutter just as in the right hands clip art, computer-made art can be brilliant.

Morgan SHEASBY / Brooklyn, New York, 16

What were your inspirations for this project?

Ice boats, hang gliders, hydroplanes, hot rods, supersonic aircraft, jet packs, Polynesian log rafts, *l'Hydroptère*, variable geometry, inflated animal skin vessels, and James Bond vehicles.

What's with the flying and boats? Is this a preoccupation of yours?

These are things that have entranced me for as long as I can remember. When I was around seven or eight years old, I used to imagine a flying rock that I could straddle, and it would take me wherever I wanted. Maybe that has something to do with the flying aspect. I grew up in the Adirondack Mountains, so my fascination with boats is a mystery. Yes, this is a preoccupation of mine.

How does passion play a part in your work?

In the craft. I think passion also mingles with obsession. For instance, on the flying ice boat piece (a.k.a. Mesopotamian Hot Rod), I wanted to make sure the sails were secured to the mast by sailor's knots, so I learned to tie bowline and camel hitch knots.

Do you love what you do?

Well, I'm never like, "Oh fuck, I've gotta make another sculpture now. Shit, man. Bummer ..."

Are you a dreamer?

I'd like to think so.

Chris THOMPSON / New York City, 20

Is lust useful?

Yes. I am driven by my desires. They give me energy and help me break through walls. Plus, they get me to do risky things—like restart my career in my thirties.

Do you consider yourself to be brave in your work?

Not at all, really. I dream about what I could do if I had no fear—if I wasn't worried about what the client or my mother would think. But I'm working on it.

What types of jobs get you excited?

Jobs with a message that I believe the world needs to hear. Unfortunately, they are also the jobs that pay the least.

Does your passionate work get you in trouble?

Sure. Passion is misread as anger. I am a very passionate person. At dinner parties, I am usually the one pounding on the table.

Chip KIDD / New York City, **22**

What were your inspirations for this project?

Some designers do paintings on the side for fun, some sculpt, others write. I have a band called Artbreak. We are pushing to finish our first self-produced album, *Wonderground*. These are some ideas for a cover, and some notes for lyrics.

Does passion play a part in your work?

You'd have to ask the passion. He seems to have a mind all his own.

Do you love what you do?

YES. *OUI. SI. DA. HAI*!!!!!!!!!

Do you feel there are enough people pursuing their lust?

I would appreciate it if (a lot) more people were pursuing their lust in my apartment.

Would pursuing this as a job make you happy?

Yes, definitely, but it's not like I'm not happy now doing everything else. What I'd like is if the music and performing (which we rarely get to do) would pay for itself. But, as long as I can afford it, that's not a big deal either. It's just so much fun to do. It is—as they say in the ads—priceless.

Kyle McDONALD / New York City, **26**

What were your inspirations for this project?

"The union of the mathematician with the poet, fervor with measure, passion with correctness, this surely is the ideal."
    —William James

How does passion play a part in your work?

"Take what's not tied down."
    —Ancient pirate proverb

"Anything worth doing is worth overdoing."
    —Mick Jagger

"If you're going to kick authority in the teeth, you might as well use two feet."
    —Keith Richards

Do you love what you do?

"I got nasty habits; I take tea at three."
    —Mick Jagger

"It's a crude world, and most people are crude. All you can do is do your best."
    —Steven Morrissey

"Age gives you a great sense of proportion. You can be very hard on yourself when you're younger, but now I just think, 'Well, everybody's absolutely mad, and I'm doing quite well.'"
    —Steven Morrissey

Are you a dreamer?

**"Lose your dreams and you might lose your mind."
—Mick Jagger**

**"When I'm lying in my bed I think about life and I think about death and neither one particularly appeals to me."
—Steven Morrissey**

KARLSSONWILKER / New York City, **28**

What were your inspirations for this project?

"The man who can't dance says the band can't play" is my favorite English saying. I would like to finally learn to dance. Lessons are being scheduled right at this moment.

How does passion play a part in your work?

Passion amplifies everything, so when I lose it, the work sucks; and when I have it, the work sucks a bit less.

Do you love what you do?

Most of the time I love what I do, and it can also happen that I love it when I actually hate it.

Do you feel there are enough people pursuing their lust?

I couldn't say. Some might not pursue it in the open, in their daily job; but maybe they do it in the closet. As long as the outlet is big enough, and fulfilling, they should be fine.

What types of jobs get you excited?

Any job where the parties involved trust and respect each other; where everyone has a backbone.

Paul SAHRE / New York City, **30**

What makes you get out of bed?

My two eleven-month-old sons. If not for them, I would for sure stay in bed much longer. And then I would also have different reasons for getting out of bed.

Do you feel there are enough people pursuing their lust?

Most of the people I am around on a daily basis are, I think.

Are you doing what you love?

Yes, at this point in time I can say that I am. Graphic design is the way I express myself. It is the way I look at the world. I feel very lucky that I live this way.

What is the ultimate job/project for you?

I don't look at the things I work on that way at all. Maybe I should be concerned that there isn't an ultimate project out there that I aspire to do. I just want to keep doing what I am doing, the way I am doing it, as long as I can.

Are you a dreamer?

No, I am a pragmatist/atheist.

Matthias EMSTBERG / New York City, **32**

Is lust useful?
Sure, we wouldn't be here/where we are without it.

Do you consider yourself to be brave in your work?
Not often enough, sadly.

What types of jobs get you excited?
A real challenge here and there gets me going.

Does your passionate work get you in trouble?
Yes, because I have a short temper.

Are you a dreamer?
Certainly yes, I am.

Jakob TROLLBACK / New York City, **34**

What were your inspirations for this project?
We almost always conceptualize our work with storyboards. The boards can be very beautiful. Sometimes you really want to move a frame or two to better the overall look, but this would obviously upset the flow and point of the story. Nevertheless, it is an intriguing setup; the boards describe time, but sometimes the different moments—or fragments—can be unstuck in time and join up to form a virtual snapshot of time.

I often think about my photography as the antithesis to my daily work. It doesn't move and it captures something still and calm. By cutting it up into 16 x 9-inch (40.6 x 22.9 cm) storyboard frames I was able to manipulate the images and add another flow that is somewhere in between a story and an expression.

How does passion play a part in your work?
I always have attempted to capture emotional moments and distill them until I understand the bare essence of the feeling they represent. These moments are like spices that we use to cook up the most fantastic suggestive experiences we can think of. In other words, it is all about passion. Without it, I believe that everything would be pointless.

Do you love what you do?
There is a lot of grunt work involved in producing media, but when it's finally done—and done well—you have created another wonderful entity that can enrich you and help you move toward the next insight.

Are you a dreamer?
Ironically, not so much. I am very much a realist, but still, creativity is my oxygen. Couldn't live without it.

Seymour CHWAST / New York City, **38**

What were your inspirations for this project?

Saul Steinberg and André François have been the inspiration for almost everything I've done.

How does passion play a part in your work?

I have a strange, unconscious drive to work. It's strange because I am naturally lazy. Passion must be a factor when I look at work I've done in the past.

Do you love what you do?

Yes.

Are you a dreamer?

24/7.

Animals often find their way into your work; is there a reason or specific way they influence you?

Animals are expressive, metaphorical, animated, symbolic, funny, engaging, sometimes evil, and sometimes angelic. They invite creative rendition, and that's why I like to use them.

Chaz MAVIYANE-DAVIES / Boston, **40**

Is lust useful?

A loaded word of biblical proportions (as in Thou shalt not lust thy neighbor's goat). My interpretation lies in a desire to deconstruct the sound bites of life that we unquestioningly appropriate and adhere to.

Do you consider yourself to be brave in your work?

Yes, but could always be braver.

What types of jobs get you excited?

All jobs that consider the human condition.

Does your passionate work get you in trouble?

Absolutely.

How dangerous are assertions/presumptions regarding graphic design?

Here are a few of my favorites:
1. The best global designers and design come out of NYC.
2. Designing a logo for a huge corporation makes you a better/more important designer than someone designing for the homeless.
3. Designing a green ad/packaging, etc., for a greedy/exploitive corporation/ institution indemnifies you from all the other things you create to help them perpetuate their practices and communication.
I could go on but I'll leave it to the *Book of Assertions* (one day).

John BIELENBERG / Belfast, Maine, **46**

What were your inspirations for this project?

The idea for this came from a group of young designers in my Project M program this summer. During the four-week-long session, we purchased an old shipping container and converted it into a mobile multipurpose studio space. I started thinking that it would be cool to have a bunch of these plopped down all over the country where we could engage young designers doing projects for the greater good.

How does passion play a part in your work?

I'm getting old and find that I have less and less tolerance for doing work I'm not passionate about. Right now, I'm most passionate about Project M.

Do you love what you do?

Most of the time ... and increasingly so!

Do you feel there are enough people pursuing their lust?

Sadly, probably not. But what do I know?

Would pursuing this as a job make you happy?

Absolutely. It's taken a long time, but I think I've finally found out what I need to do with design.

Lanny SOMMESE / Philadelphia, **48**

What makes you get out of bed?

When I was a tot my grandma Clema told me that bedsores are probable if you snooze past 7 a.m. Other than that, the need to get my kids off to school and get a good cup of coffee.

Do you feel there are enough people pursuing their lust?

It depends on how bad they want it. I've certainly tried to pursue mine. As I remember, it started slowly ... first came a yearning for a Gene Autry toy pistol and holster set followed by a yen for a Schwinn. Then a craving for Jerry West's jump shot, and finally in eighth grade, the big "L" ... LUST for a freckled, bespectacled girl named Cookie Noble. Shaking, with visions of Cookie dancing in my head, I hand-lettered "Lanny" on her notebook and "Cookie" on mine ... in cursive! Alas, my Cookie was not a cookie but a crumb with no chewy caramel center. She left me for a chunky ninth-grader.

Are you doing what you love?

Yes! After many years of self-doubt and therapy I was able to get things back on track. Over the last forty years I have pursued a lust for graphic design that began in college. Nowadays, in addition to chasing my wife around and harassing our kids and cats, I spend my time making graphic design and graphic designers.

Are you a dreamer?

Yes, and I am thankful to have found and been able to pursue mine. However, as John Lennon once wrote, "You may say that I'm a dreamer, but I'm not

the only one." These days it's wonderful to see my students realizing and accomplishing their dreams, and I'm proud to guide them on that journey.

What is the relationship between simple and powerful?
They are the same.

Matthew McGUINNESS / London, **52**

What were your inspirations for this project?
My main inspiration, for most of my recent works, has been this incredible move to another world. I moved to London [from Brooklyn] with my girlfriend, now fiancée. I moved with her not knowing how I would pull it off. Many of my recent projects have had to do with this new life (the making of a new life), her support, and the kind of love that they do not print on Hallmark cards—but the kind a father or mother would tell their son or daughter—"It's not always easy, but it's worth it!"

How does passion play a part in your work?
Without passion, it's all just a job, even one's own life.

Do you love what you do?
Some days I love what I want to do. Some days I love what I did. Some days I don't even think about it, because I am off with my lady, surfing, or so entrenched in the moment. It can be addictive when things line up.

Do you feel there are enough people pursuing their lust?
To answer this, I think of the reggae artist, Yellowman. He was diagnosed with throat cancer and had one-third of his throat removed, yet he performs with an intensity that rivals the energy of artists significantly younger than him, as if nobody told him he got sick in the first place or how he nearly died only a short while ago. I want to follow my love like that. I do not want to stop even when it looks like I have to. I want to have the conviction to make my work in the face of mortality, economics, and above all opportunity.

What types of jobs get you excited?
I absolutely love to collaborate—although some of my past collaborators may say differently after working with me, but our retrospective would prove a wonderful ride.

Neville BRODY / London, **58**

What were your inspirations for this project?
I assume the subject of lust in society to be a politicized one. It is about the loss of innocence and the hijacking of our basic emotions and hopes to better serve those in power. Joyful childhood is played out in an invisible arena of skillful message control and preconditioning.

How does passion play a part in your daily work?
What I do daily isn't what I would call work; it is passion. Work is sitting in meetings and looking at numbers.

What types of jobs get you excited?

Ones you wouldn't call jobs. I am so lucky to be doing this stuff, and there aren't enough hours to do it all.

Does your passionate work get you in trouble?

Yes, please.

Your work on these pages could have larger/social messages. Do you feel they would be relevant as posters or billboards, even though they are somewhat private?

Yes, these are private issues that we all share.

Wil FREEBORN / Gourock, Scotland, 62

What were your inspirations for this project?

It was a good opportunity to take a step back from what I normally do and think about what I'd like to do free from making a living.

I've always been a fan of travel journal illustrators such as Paul Hogarth and Ronald Searle. Especially the drawings Searle did while he was a POW in the Second World War. It's quite difficult to explain why I'd like to go to Afghanistan to draw. I think it's mostly to find out and hopefully portray in some way what life is like over there. Not the bigger picture, but the small day-to-day happenings of people in the most difficult of situations.

The other page is a desire to really knuckle down and get my life drawing better. I try and work on it twice a week, but I feel almost like I'm running out of time. I was brought up to draw "what I see," but academic drawing is more of an understanding, so you need to know anatomy. I love the specific techniques necessary to make an object look three-dimensional or real. I'm not sure why I find that so strangely mind-blowing, but I do.

How does passion play a part in your work?

Passion makes me want to do work, but it's something more calculated and dogged that gets it done.

Do you love what you do?

Yes, I'm getting there. I made a choice recently on wanting to do the work I'd like (or love) to see, and it changed how I work. I have a few projects that I'd like to see get off the ground, and I think they come from a certain love of what I do.

Are you a dreamer?

Yes, a bit of a fantasist. I like how you can throw ideas about in your head just before you sleep, where your thoughts are much more lucid. I have a pad to quickly jot them down. I wish I could think like this during the day, though it could be awkward, as it's pretty trancelike.

Your sketches have a travel journal feel. Is traveling part of your lust?

I most definitely would love to travel a lot more and come home to Scotland regularly. I'm learning French at the moment so I can spend more time traveling in France. Drawing while traveling is great fun, but it's almost impossible to draw the main tourist attractions because it's difficult to see them in a new light. It's worthwhile to search out new areas to draw, and it becomes a bit more of an adventure.

Kari PIIPPO / Mikkeli, Finland, **66**

Is lust useful?

My wife, Paula, told me years ago: "If you were a subject of open brain surgery, they would find your cranium filled with tiny little posters—and nothing else!" I took that as a compliment. Over forty years of graphic design, and I'm still excited as ever!

How do you stay fresh?

I travel a lot and I keep my eyes and mind open.

What kinds of jobs get you excited?

When the co-creators are Shakespeare, Moliére, Tšehov, and Fo—I can feel nothing but being very privileged. Designing a poster for their plays is always very exciting.

Does your passionate work get you in trouble?

When I was a young designer, conflicts happened and I lost some customers. Now I have such a position that I can carry out my vision. The customers trust my decisions since they have seen that I can give them more than they expect.

How do your surroundings influence your work?

A designer's work is always in dialogue with his own cultural environment. To be a good communicator, the designer needs to understand what happens in the world around him. Therefore, I want to be an observer: Everyday life gives the best ideas.

Fanny LeBRAS / Paris, **70**

What were your inspirations for this project?

I didn't try to express one idea in particular, or what my dream job would be. These spreads are entirely inspired by my notebook where I write and draw all my ideas, projects, hopes. Those are my current projects, works, expectations.

Do you love what you do?

Yes, to a point where I spend time drawing prosaic moments of my day, and design my own shopping lists, and my receipts. Maybe that's closer to craziness!

Are you a dreamer?

In a way, I guess. One thing I am pretty sure about: I want to move forward.

What part does your sketchbook play in achieving your lust?

I don't think it achieves it. It's a constant process to achieve my lust.

Catherine ZASK / Paris, **74**

Does your work inspire you enough to get out of bed?

Yes. Actually, it makes it difficult to go to bed.

Are you doing what you love?

Yeah!

What was the inspiration to make these beautiful pages?
To say yes to you, James.

Are you a dreamer?
Yes, indeed.

Pierre BERNARD / Paris, **76**

From where did the inspiration come for these pages?
Inspiration is very often coming from my feelings about our Earth ... our resisting Earth.

What types of jobs get you excited?
All jobs, when I feel free to think by myself.

You seem to have a "wish for the world" in this work. Is this part of your passion?
When I draw the Earth, my pleasure is that we (the human beings) are, all of us, on it!

Leonardo SONNOLI / Rimini, Italy, **78**

What makes you get out of bed?
My children; otherwise I love to sleep. But, at the end, I feel guilty.

Do you feel there are enough people pursuing their lust?
Lust is not an absolute value. It's related to the "normality" of the life. So, I think many people are pursuing their lust.

Are you doing what you love?
Not entirely. Never enough.

Would pursuing this as a job make you happy?
Not entirely. A job is really important but not the only thing.

Are you a dreamer?
I think I am.

What do you believe the differences are between art and design?
I don't care about the difference between art and design. I just like something or not. I just do something with my feeling.

Christoph NIEMANN / Berlin, **84**

Is lust useful in work?
Even though I can go a few hours just based on routine and determination, I am pretty much screwed without lust.

Do you consider yourself to be brave in your work?
I think there are two official ways of being brave as a designer, and I am neither. One is to take a chance by throwing ideas out there to the audience, without a real sense of what will happen.
I admire people who work experimentally, but I am far too obsessive and too much of a control freak to work this way (and still have a ton of ideas fall totally flat despite my efforts).

The second kind is a sort of social/political bravery. For this one, I fear I am too realistic (cynical?). I think world peace can be achieved only through education, economics, and politics. Good graphic design doesn't hurt, but I am not too optimistic about confronting the forces of evil with a witty drawing and changing their minds.

What types of jobs get you excited?

Often the most boring ones. I have to admit that it is not the assignment but rather the process and the solution that get me excited.

Does your passionate work ever get you in trouble?

Nope. I wonder if that's bad?

Are you a dreamer?

Yes, in a sense that I believe that there are amazing opportunities out there in the world, and somewhere hidden in the dark corners of my brain. No, in a sense that either can be achieved with anything else but happy, yet grinding, labor.

Max KISMAN / Amsterdam, 88

Is lust useful?

Yes. Lust stimulates focus. It also narrows generality down to particularity; and complexity to simplicity. Lust is a strong force to set, aim at, and achieve a certain goal. Lust for things, respect, love, acceptance, beauty, learning, presence, warmth, balance, taste. Lust for simplicity, yes.

Do you consider yourself to be brave in your work?

As a matter of fact, I do … and impulsive. Impulsivity is dangerous, because it ignores consequences of its actions. Or, it is plain stupid. To be brave is being kind of stupid.

What types of jobs get you excited?

The types that stimulate, enforce, and enable improvisation and experimentation to achieve unforeseen and surprising results.

Does your passionate work get you in trouble?

I don't think so. Instead, it gets me out of trouble. Passion, when recognized, is something that is highly appreciated. Whether it pays the rent is something else. In that case, it could get me in trouble ....

Are you a dreamer?

Yes, especially after eating chocolate before sleeping. I could recommend it. If dreaming is the same as fantasizing, I could be a dreamer. I sometimes like to think of things or situations, within the realm of my possibilities, that could happen. If there is enough foundation, I'll try to make it really happen.

How does connectivity increase creativity?

Connectivity is the basis for feedback. Feedback is important to criticize, judge, and balance your own views and ideas. When feedback circles around in sync, it multiplies the power of the idea. So connectivity = feedback = energy = creativity. And, vice versa.

Claudia SCHMAUDER / Zurich, **100**

What were your inspirations for this project?

Life and love and lust and me.

How does passion play a part in your work?

Addiction to the unknown leads to the passion of wandering through thoughts and pictures that are guides to results you have never expected.

Do you love what you do?

Definitely.

Are you a dreamer?

I guess. I am curious.

How important is play to your process?

Life is a great playground. Don't mess with the others in the sandbox.

Karel MISEK / Prague, **102**

Is lust useful?

What's very important for me is the sense and aim of the project, and thus also the concept, which I then follow obsessively. If it is useful, it then manifests itself in the results of my work.

    Generally speaking, lust functions as a strong source of motivation. For creative people it's a means, if not a condition, for achieving great success. But, we can well imagine all sorts of human activities—and history will give us a lot of examples of this—where lust has dreadful consequences.

Do you consider yourself to be brave in your work?

Bravery is one of the conditions of not only the work, but also the very existence of an artist. Of course, I think this about myself, but not everyone will see it like that. In any case, I am guided by the need to keep on discovering things, and so I regard new problems as a challenge. I seek out new themes and issues, which don't just interest me alone.

What types of jobs get you excited?

I particularly enjoy working on cultural and social projects, because the final product reveals them to have some kind of sense and substance to them. I worry about apathy and what is often the indifference of society in the face of suffering and also selfishness and pettiness where people should be offering their help instead. I don't just mean responses to natural disasters, I'm also referring to the general direction our civilization is going. This provides a huge scope for artists who can point the way via the position they have adopted.

Does your passionate work get you into trouble?

I'm often inflexible toward clients, which necessarily creates difficulties. My whole life I've dreamt of having enlightened clients. It's often very difficult for me to push my work through. I don't know if it's better elsewhere, but I'm afraid that, in a cultural context, our civilization isn't able to create the conditions for major works, as was the case during the Italian Renaissance, for example. Most of the products emerging now are intended only for short-

term use, and the world is being increasingly contaminated with useless things that become trash.

Your contribution for LUST deals with relationships, how do you feel they affect your work?

On the one hand, I'm an introvert and, as such, I have to have the feeling that what I do satisfies me. Of course, aesthetics is the instrument of a work's expression, but what's important are the relationships that each project creates, and its ability to communicate with individuals, the transfer of ideas.

This is a chance to realize something that is strong for me personally, and it's wonderful. Personal reflection and the confrontation of freely expressed opinions give me strong motivation to seek solutions that I can ultimately apply in my commissioned work as well.

Piotr MLODOZENIEC / Warsaw, 106

Is lust useful?

Yes.

Do you consider yourself to be brave in your work?

Yes.

What types of jobs get you excited?

Artistic.

Does your passionate work get you in trouble?

No.

What role does current events and culture play in your work?

One of the most important.

Radovan JENKO / Ljubljana, Slovenia, 108

Is lust useful?

Of course, if for nothing else, your soul.

Do you consider yourself to be brave in your work?

Never enough!

Are you a dreamer?

Yes, with bare feet.

How does contrast play a role in your work?

Like any other art tool—to make work, work.

Vladimir CHAIKA / Moscow, 112

What makes you get out of bed?

The ticktock of the clock, the flow of the time ... of my life.

Are you doing what you love?

No, to my regret.

Are you a dreamer?

Armenian anecdote: Question: Do you like tomatoes?

Answer: To eat—yes; in general—no.

Vladimir Chaika on submitting his work:

I tried to scan my pages, but the result was boring, so in order to support you, I took the photos by myself. The photo is much better, you see. I think it's nice to use photos with some concrete background frame.

Question: Why not send originals?

Because Russia is Russia! And Russian FedEx doesn't mean FedEx at all!!! They have asked a million questions about sending materials. And finally it's impossible to send!

—because it's art (please bring permission from the Ministry of Culture)
—because pornography (!)
—because I can't send flash card (necessary to confirm content)
—because they need copy of each page of my passport
—because...
— ...

Please check my files and let me know—do you still need originals? If you tell me yes, I need originals—I will try once more time to send it. Unfortunately not earlier, because we have three days of the national holidays. Waiting for your answer.
Chaika

Sadik KARAMUSTAFA / Istanbul, **120**

Is lust useful?

If you can smell and touch, lust is useful and also necessary. I am afraid we are losing our sense of smelling, touching, and holding in the digital age.

Do you consider yourself to be brave in your work?

Frankly, not always.

What types of jobs get you excited?

Work that allows me to ask contradictory questions to create new problems.

Does your passionate work get you in trouble?

Sometimes after a meeting with a client, I find myself shouting: "Fuck solution, I want to be the PROBLEM!"

Are you a dreamer?

Yes, I am. My dreams are my ideas.

Are dreams costly to pursue?

Not exactly. Dreams are precious and rare. Main problem is being able, or not being able, to recycle dreams.

Yossi LEMEL / Tel Aviv, **124**

Is lust useful in your life or work?

Without lust you die! No passion, no session ...

Do you consider yourself to be brave in your work?

In my political work, I'm trying to check borders. I'm trying to find out the limits of expression to deal with sensitive issues—painful, loaded situations—and to find surprising solutions. Yes, I still have a lot of fears I have to deal with, and I'm fighting the limitations that I put on myself.

What types of jobs get you excited?

Political, social, environmental problems make me excited and curious, and the way I break the code to get to the solution is always enthusiastic.

You have a reputation as a designer; now your work changes to photography. Is this pursuing your passion?

I always worked simultaneously with both my designer and photographer personalities. I use photography as an instrument to illustrate a concept, as someone else will use typography or illustration.

Your family seems to take a lead in your work. Can you tell me a little about that?

As a father of four, I realize the importance they play in the way I look at things, the way I look at my work, and the right proportions in life. I have this passion to get them involved in what I do, to be part of my creation, and to enjoy the experience of the process. This allows me to spend more time and explore new adventures with people that I really love—and this includes my parents.

Wang XU / Guangzhou, China, **132**

Is lust useful?

Yes, the LUST project is useful. It allows designers to think and express our own ideas.

Do you consider yourself to be brave in your work?

This project is my attempt at bravery, but I am not that self-confident.

Does your passionate work get you in trouble?

Well, more passionate work will have more trouble, and would be easier to fail.

Are you a dreamer?

No, I am not.

Ahn SANG-SOO / Seoul, Korea, **138**

below = human.
right = lives.with.four.legs.
left = lives.living.in.the.water.&.in.the.sky.
top = plants.trees.
all.is.linked.one.body.if.animal.is.sick.human.being.is.sick.
if.they.cannot.live.we.cannot.live.
if.they.are.happy.we.are.happy.
human.being.is.below.
we.respect.other.lives.
tree.on.the.head.it.is.antenna.for.receiving.message.from.universe.
under.sun.&.moon.if.all.lifes.live.in.the.right.place.
it.means.peace.
even.sun.&.moon.locate.in.the.right.position.too.

Keizo MATSUI / Osaka, Japan, **140**

What were your inspirations for this project?
We should consider the problem of the Earth where it lives now.

What types of jobs get you excited?
The unknown ones.

Is lust useful in work?
The desire becomes a factor to beat my hips. However, the state of nothing is unlimitedly and psychologically good.

I love the land mines piece.
It is hoped that the land mines disappear from the Earth some day.

Do you think design can make a difference in this cause?
There only has to be one person who feels it.

Chris BOWDEN / Adelaide, South Australia, **144**

What were your inspirations for this project?
I wanted to look back upon the things that really got me interested in designing in the first place. While I might like to imagine I was inspired by classical Swiss design and modernism, the truth is that my earliest incentives for actually doing my own creative work were things such as comic books, old Colorforms sets, and big, chunky art supplies. These are the types of things I wanted to reflect in these pieces. They are as much as a reflection of what I try to do now. I guess. I mean, who doesn't like big, chunky pieces of wood type? I've been collecting them, but I haven't found much in the way of a practical use for them. I don't think I'll be cramming a letterpress into my home anytime soon, so like my boxes of old Letraset, they're just another thing I like to hang on to. Frankly, it's been a nice excuse to get away from the computer and make a mess. Collage plays a large part in the illustrative work I do. I'm also a compulsive list maker, with scribbled patches of paper often turning up in my pockets before they go in the washing machine, or they end up as "dandruff" over all my clothes after said notes have gone through the wash.

How does passion play a part in your work?
I'm sure I'm not alone in saying that I would find some outlet for all of this even if I wasn't working as a so-called "professional designer." I'd say passion plays a large part for all of us. Nobody goes into graphic design to become a millionaire, do they? I work a fairly staid day job as a designer and spend nights and weekends working on jobs that inspire me to create and push me in interesting directions creatively. That passion can wane after a long day, but usually something will come along to reignite the spark and get me thinking about the possibilities again.

Do you love what you do?
It's a slippery slope some days, but I couldn't imagine myself really doing anything else. I've had to scratch out my own niche and comfort level in my

little hometown and reinvent myself over the years to keep working in some semblance in the industry. I've got friends I studied with who have gone on to totally unconnected careers. I guess that's not all that uncommon. I think graphic design is an infinitely interesting and growing profession that for the most part avoids the "wankery" of a lot of other professional creative outlets. Even its greatest practitioners are some of the most gracious and most humble individuals you will come across because, for the most part, they love what they do.

Are you a dreamer?

To some extent, as I get older, I'm trying more to make those dreams into realities as far as my design work goes, anyway. I've always had a very fertile "interior" world. As a kid I read a lot, drew a lot, and watched lots of TV, but I also played a lot. I was always very good at working out the scenarios with my friends, and then we would play it out. Growing up and living in a small city in the wrong part of the world, you imagine that there are endless possibilities in the big design centers and being a part of it, but the truth is that those possibilities are available anywhere if you work hard enough for them.

How do you feel about technology regarding graphic design and creativity?

I've always tried to be very "hands-on" as far as my design work goes. I like the stuff I do to have some human edge to them, to show there is a real personality behind the piece. Often the design process will start with sketches or big, chunky paintbrushes or cut paper, but it nearly always all comes together again in the computer. I don't hold rosy memories of the good old days of paste-up, drawing pens, and bromide cameras, but I'm glad I had that experience. My opinion has generally been the computer should be among the last steps, not the first. That said, it allows me to do what I do quickly and efficiently. I don't have the luxury of being a Luddite, so I'm going to use anything that I have access to, to produce what I need to get done.

Garth WALKER / Durban, South Africa, **148**

Is lust useful?

Like air or cappuccino, it's what keeps us going. We designers are all sluts at heart anyway.

Do you consider yourself to be brave in your work?

Well, it's only graphic design, and I live in Africa, so we can do things others can't. I'd like to be a lot braver. But I do publish stuff that's pretty hardcore.

What types of jobs get you excited?

Projects like this that allow me to start with a blank piece of paper—which is terrifying for a lot of designers—and do my own thing. What's not to like when you are the client?

Does your passionate work get you in trouble?

Sometimes. Usually from people who have their own agenda, and as designers, we are soft targets. In the end, no one takes design seriously—well, not at the bottom of Africa—so one shouldn't lose sleep over it.

How much do daily experiences influence your work? And do you keep a record of them?

A lot, actually, but it depends on the experience. I record much of what I like or what I find to be inspirational with photography, and have a vast collection of packaging and African street design. Much of this archive ends up in my work in one form or another.

El FANTASMAS / Argentina, **162**

Is lust useful?

In its sexual version? No, that's why we love it.

What types of jobs get you excited?

The new ones.

Does your passionate work get you in trouble?

Just economic.

Are you a dreamer?

Yes, at night.

Rico LINS / Sao Paulo, Brazil, **166**

What were your inspirations for this project?

My love for traveling, getting in touch with things I'm not familiar with, and building connections.

How does passion play a part in your work?

When I am doing something I love, I am totally on it. In most projects I jump into, I'm driven by challenge, curiosity, fantasy, seduction, and an intense exchange.

Do you love what you do?

I love what I do and wish I would only do what I love.

Are you a dreamer?

Without dreams, it would be a nightmare!

How big a role do found objects play in your work/inspiration?

When I do a collage, the found art is physically essential in all levels. For all sorts of projects, and in a more abstract way, all gathered fragments of my personal experience and repertoire—what I catch from everyday life and from people's attitudes—are among my most powerful creative sources.

Christian HELMS / Austin, Texas, **172**

What were your inspirations for this project?

My wife's parents love to say, "If it is to be, it's up to me." I love that. We designers love to complain to each other about the hassles of clients or vendors and the limitations we perceive them putting on our creativity. Our failures are nobody's fault but our own.

Does passion play a part in your work?

Absolutely. We've intentionally stayed small so that we can work with clients we love and admire rather than taking on crap projects to keep the lights on. We're also doing more and more self-initiated projects such as Frank, the restaurant, and deli grocery we've opened here in Austin.

Do you love what you do?

Every day. And I'm just getting started.

Are you a dreamer?

Yup, and I'm not the only one. I'm lucky to have an amazing network of friends out there pursuing their dreams, and I find a huge amount of inspiration in what they're doing. Whether it's with designers such as you (James) and John Bielenberg, or musicians like Will Johnson and Craig Finn, sitting down together for a beer always gets me fired up. We're all building something we love and want to see out there in the world.

Your contribution seems to have a "mission statement" feel to it. Is this part of the plan?

Definitely. No one's going to grant us permission to start the things we're dreaming of doing. Rather than thinking about the projects we wish we could work on, or the things we wish we could do with our lives, we should use that energy to make it happen. It's good to remind yourself of that, from time to time.

Art CHANTRY / Seattle, **174**

What were your inspirations for this project?

I've always lusted for the Space Needle—ever since I was a little kid, watching them build it for the 1962 Seattle World's Fair. My dad originally told me that they were going to erect it all in one piece and then use the world's largest crane to simply lift it into place. I think he believed it, too. Then came the day it was supposed to happen—he bundled up the whole family and drove down to the Seattle waterfront to see that huge crane do the work. When there was no crane, no Space Needle, no crowds, nothing, we all got mad at him for being so gullible and we drove home in a big, bickering argument. It was a grand day out in the Chantry family!

How does passion play a part in your work?

I love everything I do, even the bad stuff. It all comes out of my person, my mind, and I am the biggest Art Chantry collector out there. In fact, I have a sample of everything I've ever done (minus one or two that slipped through the cracks over the years). A publisher wants me to do a book including everything—all in small reproductions set up like a huge postage-stamp collector album. I intend to follow through on it, but it takes time and money to put something like that together. I gotta make a living, ya know ....

Are you a dreamer?

I'm an iconoclast and nihilist and, (at heart), an idealist, but not a dreamer.

Your new house looks strangely like the Space Needle. Is this part of your world domination?

If I were the richest man in the world, I would buy the Space Needle, for sure. I would move in and make it my permanent residence. I would want everybody in the world to drive by that cool-looking weird-ass building and point and say, "That's where the richest man in the world lives!"

That's the problem with this nouveau riche class of micro-yuppies. They've got no imagination. They don't know how to spend their money. Why hasn't Bill Gates or Paul Allen purchased the needle to live in? They bought everything else in Seattle! Why not the Space Needle?

Rick VALICENTI / Chicago, **180**

What were your inspirations for this project?

The polarized world of dysfunctional behavior that drags us all to the abyss of hateful rhetoric and despicable acts. This project represents the schwing of my pendulum.

How does passion play a part in your work?

Come on! That is like asking an astronaut how rocket fuel factors into space travel. Passion is the only gift I have that really fuels everything. Without it, all I treasure would be clouded over with a thick yuck. Doing work is the only way I say thank you to my passion for being there all along.

Do you love what you do?

I love to get lost in the space at the intersection of making and thinking where a ringing phone has yet to be invented.

Are you a dreamer?

Indeed! Yet, the dreams I have when my eyes are closed seem to vanish when the alarm sounds. Maybe I need to write them down just before they vaporize entirely.

399073

399073